Everything Is Going To Be All Right

A true story based on Jeremiah 29:11

Rev. Dr. Robert S.J. Coutts

ISBN 978-1-64515-476-1 (paperback)
ISBN 978-1-64515-477-8 (digital)

Christian Faith Publishing, Inc.
832 Park Avenue
Meadville, PA 16335
www.christianfaithpublishing.com

Printed in the United States of America

"For I know the plans I have for you," declares the Lord,
"plans to prosper you and not to harm you,
plans to give you hope and a future."

—Jeremiah 29:11 (NIV)

CONTENTS

INTRODUCTION

Jeremiah 29:11 says, "For I know the plans I have for you, declares the LORD, plans to prosper you and not to harm you, plans to give you hope and a future." You would think that the average person would read those words and know that God has our best interest at heart and that He wants to guide our lives. Reading those words conjures up a feeling of everything will be okay because God is in control. However, we do not all think that way. We tend to worry a lot or be concerned about our lives when things go wrong.

If Scripture elicits that type of response from many, how much more disconcerting is it when someone other than God tells you everything is going to be all right? The first reaction is to be skeptical. How would they know, you ask? What inside information do they have? Did someone show them your future? Maybe somebody told you everything was going to be all right, and in the end, it wasn't. You haven't walked a mile in my shoes. Your sickness is not like my sickness. That could tend to deflate your faith process. But take heart. When you know God, you do not need to be concerned about someone telling you how things will turn out. Rather, you just need to know that with God, everything will be all right.

As I was growing up, I heard that saying many times. The very first time was as an eleven-year-old boy in the form of a dream or an epiphany, if you will. Later I will describe a dream which involved Jesus speaking directly to me and telling me, "Bob, everything's going to be all right!" After having that dream, God performed one miracle after another, leading to where we are today. It is definitely a story of hope and encouragement for any who are in despair or facing one of life's harsher challenges. Through this story, I hope to be able to encourage you. Some of the things that happened in my early years are atrocious. Some are phenomenal. God was always there.

If you are wondering what is to become of you because of the situation you are in now, then you need to know what I found out. Your life is in His hands, and God never fails, nor does He forget you. Looking back, I can see the hand of God at every turn, and seeing that hand move for me has moved me to write to encourage others who may be in a similar situation. God never leaves us and never forsakes us.

I am hoping this reflection will bring hope and encouragement to those who read it. God has seen fit to put His hand on my life and take me on an incredible journey from abuse and separation to reunion and forgiveness that was undeniably God planned and executed. All along the way, many lives have been touched in ways that only eternity will reveal.

He said in Psalms 138:8, KJV, *"I will perfect the things that concern you. My mercy endures forever. I will not forsake the work of my hands."*

I pray that any who read these words will first and foremost find Christ as their Savior and see that they are not alone in their walk to eternity. For others, I trust it will encourage them to know that with God, *everything's going to be all right.* Some might call this a memoir, and that's okay. If the story behind my life causes anyone to find hope in God, then it was worth the time taken to write it.

CHAPTER 1

Early Life

A Look Back

God has done such a tremendous work in my life that it is hard to know where to start. There are so many things that have happened since the date of my birth, and they all point to God. If I needed a starting point, the place where it all began, then I guess I would need to start at the age I have my first recollection, and that would be at age two and a half because those are very impressionable years, and also God already had His protecting hand on me then.

Robert (Bobby) Coutts, age two and a half

First of all, let me give you a little sense of who I am and where I came from. I am now a minister who has retired from full-time pastoring but continue in as much ministry as the Lord affords me daily. I grew up as a child of a serviceman and moved around to quite a few air force bases. I received good schooling and did well in my classes. At birth, I was a twin, but my twin sister was stillborn. Mom and Dad raised five children. The oldest, my sister Susan, has passed from this life, and three sisters and I remain. I was the second born, and I have a sister that is twenty years my junior. There is no contact with two of those sisters, but I do have a good relationship with the second youngest, who is also a born-again Christian. Unfortunately, the home I come from was an abusive one. If you can name the abuse, I suffered it. I will not go into much depth concerning it because I believe in so doing, it just tends to give the devil a stage, and that is not going to happen. I will cover a few examples only because they are pertinent to seeing them as God allowing such things as part of His plan to use me later in life.

My life has been marked with many of the things that people face daily: love, hate, suffering, sickness, poverty, hard work, and family, just to name a few. As this story unfolds, it will cover some of those things and share with you the amazing hand of God throughout. My Bible tells me to remember the Creator in the days of my youth.

> *Remember now thy Creator in the days of thy youth, while the evil days come not, nor the years draw nigh, when thou shalt say, I have no pleasure in them.* (Ecclesiastes 12:1, KJV)

Perhaps the reason for that would be to remember all the wonderful things God has done so that perhaps they can be shared with others and hopefully be an encouragement to them.

One of the first things I can remember is at the age of two and a half, sitting on my grandfather's lap and him telling me stories. I couldn't tell you what those stories were now for the life of me, but I remember I felt safe and loved.

Grandpa and Grandma
Robert Alfred and Violet Wilhelmina Coutts

You see, my dad was an abusive alcoholic. He did not need an excuse to whip me. He just needed the courage or a drink. I never sat on my own father's lap, nor did he ever tell me a story. When I got older and a little more grown up, Dad would drink and tell me stories that were so off-color that you would need a new name for the color. He must have thought I was "mature enough" to hear them. Dad was military all the way. He had joined the army, and even then, he had lied about his age to get in. He and his brother went to Germany and Italy and served out their time together there during World War II. When they came back, booze became an escape. Today when a person comes back from some skirmish abroad, they call what they have when they get back PTSD, or post-traumatic stress disorder. Each has their own way of coping with it, and Dad's and his brother was booze. Dad's brother's drinking was so bad that his wife, my aunt, had enough and shot herself, committing suicide. Dad continued on in the army. He jumped to the 48th Highlanders and then into the Royal Canadian Air Force in 1952. He remained in the air force until

1969 when he finally decided service life was enough, and he retired from it. But needless to say, Dad was a drunk, and a mean one at that. So at two and a half, the safe spot for me was on my grandpa's lap.

I spent a lot of time at Grandpa and Grandma's house. Mom and Dad were too busy for me, so summers were set aside to stay at the grandparents' place. Don't get me wrong, Grandpa was not about no discipline either. But the difference between him and my father was how he handled me during and after the discipline.

Grandpa's Love

Here's an instance of Grandpa's love. Grandpa had a Model A Ford—a beautiful, shiny black two-door one—and he was outside shining that car all the time.

Replica of Grandpa's Model A Ford

One day my sister and I were playing outside, and we got it in our heads that we would like to go for a ride in Grandpa's car. So we went in the house and asked Grandpa if he would take us. Well, Grandpa was sleeping in his chair, and I guess he just did not want to be disturbed because he grunted out a no. Susan (my "older" sister) and I persisted, and we asked again. Grandpa was a bit annoyed, and he just opened his eyes and plainly said, "Sorry, there is no gas in the car, so I am going to have a sleep. Go out and play." Well, Susan and

I were not deterred by his "I have no gas" story, so we proceeded to get the garden hose and our little kids' beach buckets. We filled the buckets with sand and poured it into his gas tank, and to make sure it filled up okay, we stuck the garden hose in the gas opening and filled it with water until all the sand washed down into the tank and the water gushed out the spout.

Then (yes, you know what's coming, don't you?) we went in and woke Grandpa and proudly stated, "Grandpa, you can take us for a ride now because you have lots of gas." I don't think it registered right away because he just grunted and said nothing, so we told him again, "Grandpa, you have lots of gas because we filled it for you. Please take us for a ride." Well, you never saw a man move as fast as my grandfather moved. He was out of that chair and outside before we could even say "wait for us." We ran outside giggling because we thought, *Yippee, he is going to take us for a ride.*

When we got out side, he was beside the car holding the hose (which we had left in the gas spout), and he was shouting and jumping around and saying words I can't or will not even spell here.

Then the unthinkable happened. He said, "Wait here!" Let me rephrase that. He did not say it; he shouted at the top of his lungs, "WAIT HERE!" I think it was at that moment that Susan and I knew something was wrong. Grandpa went down the path to the brook beside our pig barn, and we saw him cutting a long switch, and we knew what it was for because we had been exposed to it once before. Needless to say, Grandpa was about to apply the board of education to our seats of learning, which he did. He said, "Bend over!" We did, and very quickly it was *whack, whack, whack,* and it was over—for him, that is! We screamed like we were murdered, and I tell you, if you have ever had a switch applied to your backside, you know what I am talking about. The difference between him and my dad was he smacked us three times each. Dad would hit until he had spent his anger.

Well, like I said, Grandpa was not one to shy away from discipline; but unlike my father, his discipline came with a difference. Grandpa applied the discipline to our butts, and it was done, and then he spent the next two days removing the gas tank and cleaning it out. He was not mean to us, nor did he continue with a tirade of anger. He smacked us, and it was over. He treated us like normal kids, but during those two days that he was repairing the damage, Susan and I stayed our distance from him. We obeyed and did what we were told but still kept a distance.

When he was all done and the car was running again, Grandpa called Susan and me outside to his watermelon garden. He said, "Come and sit down." We did, and Grandpa said this: "Bobby, Susan, I love you with all my heart. What you did was wrong, and that is why I spanked you." Then Grandpa took a big knife and cut a huge watermelon right down the middle and handed us two spoons and said, "I love you both, and I hope you understand why I spanked you. If you want to go for a ride in the car, let me gas it up, not you." Then he sat down in the garden with us and pulled out a spoon and helped us eat the watermelon. Then he took us for a ride in his shiny new black Model A Ford! That night, I was sitting on my grandfather's lap again—safe and loved! *Train up a child in the way he should go: and when he is old, he will not depart from it"* (Proverbs 22:6, KJV).

My grandfather was constantly on my father's case about how he treated me and continually beating me, especially when he had been drinking, but it did not stop Dad. The booze spoke for him, and I guess he just didn't understand the influence of it. The drinking and the beatings continued.

Beginning of Sorrows

Dad reenlisted in the service, and we moved away from my grandparents' house about three hours away to another Royal Canadian Air Force base called Trenton, Ontario.

Dad (George R. Coutts) in the service

We did not see my grandparents much after that other than birthdays, Easter, a couple of weeks in the summer when we would go and stay with them, and then Christmas, when they would come to visit. The next five years after moving away from the grandparents' would shape my life and start a time of systematic abuse, mental, physical, and sexual. They were turbulent years and left me with a lot of fears, anger, superstitions, and anxieties that would take years to recover from.

The first visit back to my grandparents' place just about cost me my life. We arrived in the middle of a summer afternoon. We were going to stay for two weeks, and I was totally excited. I would get to climb his seventy-foot oak tree (if Dad saw me do it, I usually got a licking for it, but I loved that tree; and maybe at the time, I thought the spanking was worth climbing the tree). I would get to sit in the pear tree and eat till I burst, pick cherries off his cherry tree, chase the pigs and chickens and fish in the creek on his property. It promised to be a wonderful time.

The very afternoon we arrived, I ran up and hugged both Grandma and Grandpa because I was so excited to see them and immediately headed for the railing that was built on their porch. It was a favorite climbing spot for me when I was at their place, and I would try walking on top of the rail like a tightrope. Grandma said, "You get down from there before you fall down on your head." It was about six feet to the ground. Not two seconds later, I fell. I woke up three days later in the hospital with my head bandaged and bruises all over my body. My grandmother was at my side, and when I came to, she said, "We nearly lost you!" Then she hugged me. Mom and Dad weren't there, and I guessed it was because they were busy working. I found out later that they had stopped in to see if I had awakened yet or not, and then the two of them headed off for the legion. I guess some things in life are more important than others.

Well, it did not end there. I got out of the hospital a few days later and went to my grandparents' place to recuperate. I was not allowed outside for a few days because of the head injury. The concussion was bad enough that I was out for a few days, and they wanted to make sure there were no relapses after I got out, so I stayed indoors under Grandma's watchful eye. That was not a bad thing because she was constantly baking. I tried green tomato pie (don't laugh—the way Grandma baked it made it taste like apple pie!). She gave me fresh baked cookies, homemade fudge, and her special peanut brittle. So staying in wasn't all that bad.

By the middle of our last week staying at their house, I was told I could go out but not to do anything strenuous. I did exactly what I was told. The weather had changed from hot to damp and cool. It was July, and that was probably unusual for that time of the year. I stayed outside all day and then back out the next day for more. By the end of the second day of being outside in the damp weather, I began to sniffle; and on the morning of the third day, I was in a full-blown cold. But it was worse than that; I was burning up and hacking my lungs out. They took me back to the hospital, and I was admitted right away. I had pleurisy and pneumonia. My system was so run-down from the earlier accident that I caught the first thing that came along and could not fight it off. I was immediately put in an iron lung because that is what they used back then to combat the pneumonia. It was touch and go for about a week, and then I started to improve.

Mom and Dad had gone back to their jobs, and I was left in the care of Grandma and Grandpa. They stayed at my side the whole time. Finally I was well enough to go home, and I went to my grandparents' place and spent another week there. Then I was returned home to Trenton in August only to be greeted with disdain. I was yelled at for getting sick. I should have known better. I was a fool. I did not obey. I brought it on myself.

Yes, this was the beginning of sorrows.

CHAPTER 2

A God Thing

Looking back on those times at my grandparents' and being in the hospital, I now know it was the hand of God on me. I didn't know it at the time; how could I? I wasn't old enough to understand, and further, no one told me that God would help me or watch over me. But He did. I did not know that later in life, God would use me in ways that I could not dream of. He had a plan for my life, and He was making me ready to receive it. I did not die from the fall on my head. I did not die from the pneumonia. I was in His hands the whole time, even if it was unbeknownst to me. After all, did not God say,

> For He shall give His angels charge over you, To keep you in all your ways. In their hands they shall bear you up, lest you dash your foot against a stone. (Psalms 91:11–12, NKJV)

A Pattern of Abuse

Things began to change after we had moved away from my grandparents' house. Dad was back in the air force, and Mom decided to quit work and just stay home and look after us kids. The first year we were in our new home in Trenton, things seemed to run smoothly. Dad would work all week and then come home and pack up his fishing gear and get up early Saturday morning, and he and his buddies would take off for a day of fishing. I was "too young" to go. "Maybe next year" was the catchphrase. So I would suffice myself to take my fishing pole and go down to the creek about a hundred yards from the house. No one told me it was a ditch and a runoff from the excess road water. But I wouldn't have cared if I was told because I would spend hours walking along the "ditch" and try to catch minnows, tadpoles, or frogs. It was those times that gave me the love for fishing. It became, over the years, as an adolescent a time of freedom and escape from the abuse suffered at home.

The second year in Trenton saw some major changes. I started school, and Dad got worse with his drinking.

Bobby at the first day of school

By now he was well known on the air base and well liked for that matter. He was elected president of the corporals club on the base, and that required him to be at the club every night. He would need to stay and close up when the bar closed at 1:00 a.m. And he would usually get home about 1:30 to 2:00 a.m. It had its benefits though. At least at the time, I thought they were benefits, until I found out that what he was doing was illegal. After he would close up, he would gather up the food from the buffet table and pack it home with him. We would eat roast beef, gravy, turkey, ham, potatoes, and such on a regular basis. He was supposed to put all the excess food back in the club's fridge for the next night, but he would stay late enough so that he could sneak it out. We ate very good until he was caught, and they put a stop to it. Surprisingly, he never was reprimanded for it, and he continued on as president as well. It makes you wonder if crime pays! Not!

It was during the time Dad was serving as president of the club that the abuse escalated from the physical beatings. Because he was always out so late at night, my mother developed a fear of being alone. That fear was translated to action. The action she took was to keep me up to all hours with her for company. We had one of those newfangled round screen TVs, and it would be on as long as the one channel was available. Mom would watch movies all night, and in particular, she would watch ungodly (then it was not deemed as ungodly) things like *Count Dracula, The Hound of the Baskervilles, Frankenstein, Sherlock Homes,* and anything that was scary to a little boy. She would have me make pot of tea after pot of tea, and I would sit up with her and watch those movies and drink tea with her. My one-year-older sister and my four-year younger sister would go to bed, and I would be kept up. I don't know if she thought because I was a male, I would make a difference to whatever calamity might befall her or not. But I stayed up with her anyway and watched TV and made tea.

Yes, I watched my share of scary stuff, and I learned a lot of stuff I did not need to learn. There were many superstitions associated with those movies, and Mother knew them all and taught me each one. For instance, crows. The saying was, "One for sorrow, two for joy, three for a girl, and four for a boy." "If you saw a murder of crows, you were going to have company." "Don't spill the salt, or you are going to get into a fight." "Don't walk on a sidewalk crack, or you will break your mother's back'." "Don't let a black cat walk in front of you, or it is bad luck." There were so many more that it would take years and years and a visitation of the Holy Spirit to deliver me from them.

But that was not the worst of it. Mom would keep me up until she saw the headlights of the car coming in the driveway and then shoo me off to bed. The bad part of it was Dad would come in the house, and somehow he knew I had been up, and usually he was drunk and come into my room. And without even asking my mom why I was up, he would proceed to paddle my backside and yell at me that I shouldn't be up so late. It became a ritual. It seems to me this was the height of hypocrisy because the sad thing was my mother did not defend me. She was afraid of him as well when he got drunk. I had seen him hit her a few times, and he was usually drunk then as well.

Life went on like this for some time, and the drinking increased, and the abuse was getting worse. Now Dad progressed to using a belt with me standing with my hands against the basement wall. Back in those days, it was considered discipline and corporal punishment. Today it is just plain old abuse.

Next we moved from Trenton air base to North Bay air force base, and that is when things (as if they couldn't) did get worse. I was getting older, and because I was receiving so many beatings from his drunken stupors, I became more rebellious. The more I rebelled, the worse it got. But some great things happened in the next two years that would have an effect on my future life even though I did not know it at the time.

Let me tell you how some of the things that happened led to an epiphany with God. I was ten years old now, and I was growing fast. I looked a lot older because of my size. I would wear through clothes very fast because of the growing spurts, and my parents had trouble keeping shoes on my feet. I would either wear them out or grow out of them very rapidly. I would wear them out because I was constantly out fishing, and I would wear the only shoes I had, and they would wear out from the rocks and water. I would sneak out of the house in the summertime very early in the morning, usually around 6:00 a.m. My friend and I would take off for our favorite creek and fish all day for speckled trout. We would stay out until 6:00 and 7:00 p.m. and then make our way home with the fish. What is wrong with this and ironic is that I would get a beating for being gone all day without telling them where I was, and then they would eat the fish I caught! I think there is a problem there somewhere!

As I was closing out my tenth year, Dad changed a lot. I was sleeping one night, and it was extremely hot. Mom and Dad came into my room and opened a window and then removed my blankets. It woke me, but I pretended I was still asleep because I was frightened and thought I might have done something to precipitate a beating. There was no beating, but this was something they had never done. I was not sure what was happening, but I remember my mother saying to my dad, "He is sweating." Dad said, "Yeah," and reached over and took my underwear off and said, "Maybe that will help cool him off." They both stood there for a moment, and Mom said, "Let's go." Dad said, "I will be down in a minute." Mom left the room and went downstairs.

Then my father did something that literally scared me half to death. It was all I could do to stay pretending that I was asleep. He sat down on the edge of the bed and began to rub his hands over my body and touch my private parts. I did not understand what he was doing, but I know it scared me. Maybe I thought he was just checking to see if I had cooled off or not, but when he touched my privates, I nearly screamed out loud because of the reaction my body gave to him touching me there. Then he stopped, got up, and went downstairs. I lay there for what seemed like an eternity crying because of the strange things happening in my body that I did not understand, and inside me something told me this was not right. And being as scared as I was, I guess the outlet was to cry and fall asleep that way.

Needless to say, this was the beginning of a new nightmare. Dad would come into my room many times and do it all over again. All he ever did was touch me, and when my body reacted, he would leave—that is, until! Until he decided one weekend that he was going to take me fishing, and we were going to camp overnight. It was only the second time he had ever taken me fishing with him.

Without going into detail, suffice it to say that we did go, and the weekend was very cold. I ended up in his sleeping bag because he said it was the best way to keep me warm. I smelled the alcohol on his breath and could feel his intentions as he curled up against me. Please don't try to guess what happened, just know that it did! Needless to say, it was the most frightening experience of my young life; and because he was drunk, he must have thought it was okay.

He warned me to keep my mouth shut or suffer the consequences. I was obedient and kept my mouth shut and told no one because I was already getting enough beatings as it was, not to mention the fact of how embarrassed I was at what he had done.

This pattern of abuse and beatings continued while we were living in North Bay, Ontario. It was here that the abuse took a different turn.

We were living in the air force PMQs (primary married quarters) on the air base—that is, housing for married couples. We had young neighbors all around us, and Mom and Dad got to know them well. The lady on one side of us would babysit us, as did the neighbor on the other side. While we were living here, Mom took sick and was hospitalized for quite some time with deteriorating disc disease. She required many surgeries to put screws in her spine just to allow her to function. The two ladies from either side of where we lived would come and help out and even spend a lot of time at our house while Mom was in the hospital. Dad was very friendly with them, and one of them, when her husband was away on some course the air force wanted him to take, came and spent many nights at the house.

I guess knowing what I know now, Dad was having an affair with both of them. I walked in on them one afternoon, and it was explained to me that he was "making her feel better because she was hurting." About a week later, Dad had to stay on the base all weekend, so the neighbor came and stayed at the house to look after me and my two sisters. Late in the evening, when we kids were all in bed, the neighbor lady came to my room and questioned me about what I had seen between her and my dad. When I could not tell her what I thought it was, she asked me if I wanted her to show me, but I was not allowed to tell anyone about what she was going to show me. The rest is history, and now I had two people who were using me in ways that are not allowed. Look what the Word says about that!

And whoever receives and accepts and welcomes
one little child like this for My sake and in My
name receives and accepts and welcomes Me.

But whoever causes one of these little ones who believe in and acknowledge and cleave to Me to stumble and sin [that is, who entices him or hinders him in right conduct or thought], it would be better (more expedient and profitable or advantageous) for him to have a great millstone fastened around his neck and to be sunk in the depth of the sea.

Woe to the world for such temptations to sin and influences to do wrong! It is necessary that temptations come, but woe to the person on whose account or by whom the temptation comes! (Matthew 18:5–7, Amplified Bible, Classic Edition [AMPC])

Up until now, I was in a state of fear all the time. If it were not Dad, it would be the neighbor. I did not dare tell anyone because of the threats from Dad, and who would believe a little kid anyway? What was I going to do?

I turned eleven, and I was quite active in sports and an active outside kid. But inside I was small and frightened all the time.

An Epiphany

Just as I turned eleven, some things began to happen that would signal a change in my life for the better, even though I did not know it at the time. I was lying in bed asleep, and I had a dream. You can chock it up to a foolish kid's dream if you want, but this dream was about to shape my life, and what happened in the dream would draw connections later that year and then again in my twenty-fifth year. We will come to that later. God just seems to have a way of putting a plan together that defies human logic.

> For my thoughts are not your thoughts, neither are your ways my ways, saith the Lord. For as the

heavens are higher than the earth, so are my ways higher than your ways, and my thoughts than your thoughts. For as the rain cometh down, and the snow from heaven, and returneth not thither, but watereth the earth, and maketh it bring forth and bud, that it may give seed to the sower and bread to the eater; So shall my word be that goeth forth out of my mouth: it shall not return unto me void, but it shall accomplish that which I please, and it shall prosper in the thing whereto I sent it. (Isaiah 55:8–13, KJV)

So there I was, sleeping. And in this dream, I heard a very loud noise. I could not recognize it, but it sounded like a freight train. Sure enough, the noise got louder and louder, and it sounded like it was coming right up the stairs outside my room. The next thing I knew, this enormous truck the likes of which I had never seen before, came right up the stairs and in through my doorway and stopped at the foot of my bed. There was a man in the driver's cab with a yellow hard hat on, and when the truck came to a stop, the man poked his head out of the driver's-side window and, with his hand, took his yellow hard hat off and waved it in the air. And with a beautiful smile that made me warm all over and made me smile inside, he said, "Bobby, everything's going to be all right." Then he put his yellow hard hat back on and backed his truck out the door of my bedroom and down the stairs and was gone.

He may have been gone at that moment, but not too far because from that moment on, it started a chain of events. The first event was Fulton J. Sheen.

The Bishop Fulton J. Sheen Connection

The reason I bring Bishop Sheen into the picture is because of the influence he had on my life. Also the man had such a towering and commanding presence that you could not help but listen to him.

REV. DR. ROBERT S.J. COUTTS

I had been watching Bishop Fulton J. Sheen on the television every chance I could because the things he said and the way he talked to children made me feel exactly like the man in the truck made me feel when he told me everything would be all right.

I look back now, and I remember I loved watching Superman and Batman shows on TV because they were the epitome of strong, and they wore capes! Well, Bishop Sheen had a cape draped over his shoulders as part of the robe he wore, and maybe I was making a connection with the capes and superpowers that I believed they all had. Hey, I was a kid, and back then we looked up to those role models.

Bishop Fulton J. Sheen, 1895–1979

Bishop Sheen was a role model to me. Dad would make fun of me watching him on the television, but I didn't care. And besides, we were a captive audience anyway because we only had one channel on the television, and you either watched it or turned it off. I was allowed to watch because as my dad said, "Maybe that guy can speak some sense into your head."

Well, I said that to say this. On Fulton Sheens program, he had a portrait or an artist's rendering of Jesus on the wall of his study. The same man in the picture, Jesus, was the same man, exactly to a tee, driving the truck! Coincidence? I think not.

Saved by Grace

> *For it is by grace you have been saved, through faith—and this is not from yourselves, it is the gift of God—not by works, so that no one can boast.* (Ephesians 2:8–9, NIV)

That dream sustained me through many more beatings and abuse. I would constantly think about Him (Jesus) telling me everything was going to be all right. It seemed I was becoming immune to the abuse until one night in particular. It was a Saturday, about two months after the dream. I had gotten up early, and I went fishing. I had gotten into the habit of telling my parents where I was going and how long I would be so I wouldn't face a licking when I got home. This time, I was so excited because my friend and I had discovered a new fishing hole that produced eight-inch speckled trout, and we were heading there that day that I forgot to tell my parents where it was and how long I would be. We got home at 6:00 p.m. with a large string of speckled trout and all excited because it was the best catch of the summer.

Dad met me at the door and began his drunken tirade about me not telling them and on and on, and then he said, "Get down the basement." I knew what was coming. It had become his habit of taking me down the basement to give me a beating. I guess it was so the noise of my crying and the crack of the belt didn't disturb anyone else in the house. So I went down, and he told me to drop my drawers and turn around with my hands on the wall. He took off his leather belt and began a frenzied whipping on my bare butt. This was the worst one yet, and he just seemed not to be able to stop. My mother was down the basement with us, and she literally had to drag him off me. I was left lying on the floor with welts up and down my legs and across my backside and crying uncontrollably. I was told to get dressed and get upstairs for supper. Can you imagine? I go fishing. Catch the fish. Come home to a beating. Then everyone sits down and eats the fish I caught. I know. It does not make sense to me either, other than booze does strange things to people.

Here is the good that came out of it. Yes! I said *good!* The next morning was Sunday, and I got up to go to the Sunday school I had started to go to about six months earlier. It was a Methodist Sunday school, and they were meeting in our school on the air base. I was allowed to go because, once again, in the words of my parents, "maybe it will do you some good."

Well, I got up and dressed. I had to wear shorts because all my pants were in the wash to be done that day. Sunday was always wash-day for my mother. So I put the shorts on, and it was then I realized that you could see all the bruises and welts down my legs. I was embarrassed, but I didn't care because I loved that Sunday school, and I was going in spite of the circumstances.

When I arrived, I was greeted by the married couple who were teaching my class. They were Methodists. The woman saw my bruises and asked if everything was okay, or had I hurt myself? She immediately recognized what had happened, and she reached over and hugged me tight. I was crying because here was someone who cared, and they were showing actual concern for me. Together, she and her husband took me to a class by myself and asked me what happened. I told them the story, and when I was done, they said there was not really that much they could do about it. But if I would let them, they would tell me about a Man who was also beaten for no apparent good reason as well. He was hated by many and even hated so much that they killed Him on a cross. But He did not stay dead. He rose again so that people like me could have a wonderful life and eventually go to heaven to be with Him forever. All I had to do was accept Him as my personal Savior and invite Him into my heart, where He would live forever.

Right then and there, they led me to Jesus. I said the sinner's prayer, and such a feeling of peace and warmth and love came over me that nothing else in the world mattered. I think at that age, I had a little understanding mixed with the need for someone to love me. When they told me that Jesus loved me, I latched on to it. Then (remember the truck and the dream?) the two of them said something to me that made me shiver all over and smile like I was going to burst. They said, "Bobby, everything's going to be all right." Exactly the same words the man (Jesus) in the truck said to me that night. I remembered it instantly, and my heart leaped inside.

Then they gave me a pocket version of the New Testament. It was provided by the Gideons International. Printed in the back was the sinner's prayer and a place for you to sign and date it when you accepted Christ.

I signed it, dated it June 15, 1959!

Now it is 2019, and I still have it, a little worn, but a great treasure.

My New Testament

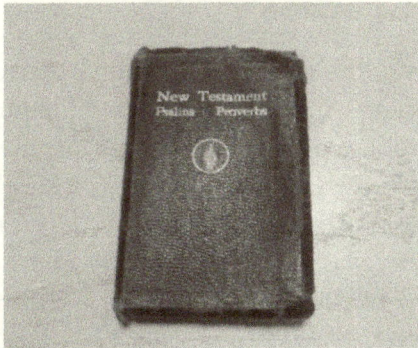

This little book is one of the greatest treasures I own. It is not the size of it that is unique. It is the size of the *words* contained inside. This little book changed me forever!

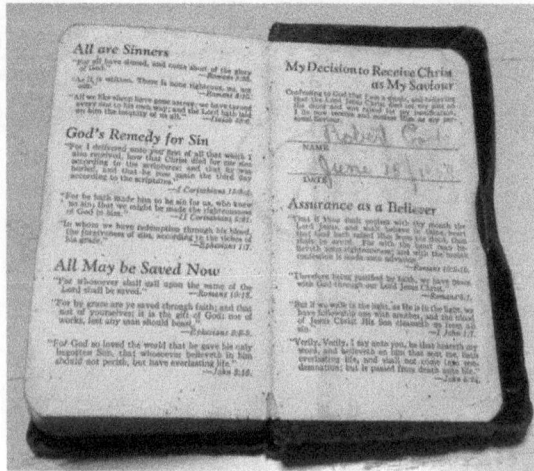

Signed June 15, 1959, accepting Jesus as my Savior

The Change

Well, things didn't seem to be getting better over the next few days until something happened that started the proverbial ball rolling. I had done something that must have made my mother so angry that she would not even give me a licking. Instead, she said, "Your father will need to take care of this one." Well, he came home drunk, and all I remember was my mother telling him how I had hit my sister, and he flew off the handle. No one asked me my side of the story. I was not even allowed to explain. Now Dad was confronting me without even listening to what I have to say. I was standing in the hall, and he came over to me and picked me up by the front of my shirt and slammed me against the wall. The wall broke, and I was halfway into the living room from the hall. He pulled me out of the wall and punched me in the face and knocked me out.

I was out for a few minutes, and when I came to, Mom and Dad were sitting at the table in the kitchen. She was crying, and he was yelling at her. They didn't see me get up and go out the door. It was late afternoon, and I thought, *I am going to run away. But I'm only eleven. Where am I going to go?* I grabbed a blanket off our swing set on the porch and ran next door and hid under their porch. It was closed in with a little hole by the steps to crawl under, so I crawled under where no one could see me. I cried myself to sleep, and when I woke up, it was dark. I peeked out, and what I saw frightened me so bad I just stayed under the neighbor's porch. There were two MP cars in our yard. That's military police from the air force base. One of the policemen was right on the step above me, talking to our neighbor, and he asked her if she had seen me. It was then I knew I was going to really get a beating when I went home. I was so scared that I just stayed under the porch until the MP left and everyone went in the house. I fell asleep again, and I must have been so tired or extra scared because I did not wake till morning. And when I looked out, there was an MP car in the yard and a lot of other cars as well. I recognized one of the cars as my grandfather's and figured they must have called him, and he made the four hour trip from Toronto when I did not come home.

I was absolutely starving right now and did not know what to do. Just then, I saw my grandfather come around the side of our house, and I guess it was to have a cigarette because I saw the flame flicker and then a cloud of smoke from his mouth. As soon as I saw him, I thought if I can get to him before my dad catches me, I would be safe. I crawled out from under the porch and ran as fast as I could to him, and he grabbed me and hugged me and told me to get in his car, and do you know what he said? He said, "Bobby, everything is going to be alright." *Wow!* Three times. It must be true. Well, it was.

Grandpa went and got Dad, and Dad tried to get to me, but Grandpa had locked me in the car and told me to not open it for anyone but him, not even Dad. I was terrified when Dad tried to get the door open, but Grandpa and Dad yelled at each other a lot, and finally Dad went in the house. Then Dad must have called the MPs because they came right back and talked to Dad and Grandpa, and then they left. They did not even talk to me or ask me why I ran away; they just left. I think they may have been friends of Dad's and knew what was going on. Well, they may not have asked me why I ran away, but I sure told my grandfather!

After all the yelling and threats from my father and my grandfather refusing to let my dad near me to beat me, Grandpa put a bunch of my clothes in a bag, and we headed for his house in Highland Creek near Toronto. I stayed with them for just over a year, and a schoolteacher (I guess you call them a tutor) came to the house to help me keep up with my school year because I was not eligible to go to a school in the district my grandfather lived in. The next year saw no beatings or abuse. I was asked by my grandfather to keep what had happened to me to myself and never talk about it because it would only hurt others. I think I understand what my grandfather was driving at, but today my advice would be to say something to someone if you have been abused.

I am thinking my grandfather must have read some kind of riot act to my father because in that year, Dad would call Grandpa's place a few times a month. He was only allowed by my grandfather to talk to me for a few minutes each time, and when he did talk to me, he would talk to me differently. I think back now and the way he talked, it was probably him trying to cover his tracks and make up to me in case I decided to talk to the "wrong people" about what he had done.

After that time at my grandparents', they felt everything had calmed down to the point I could go home. Dad never touched me again, nor did he beat me anymore. Maybe my grandfather's "talk" with him worked. But on the other side of the coin, he made a point to avoid me as much as possible and never took me anywhere and was never alone with me. It was like he was shutting me out of his life or protecting himself from himself. He still yelled at me, but not like it was before.

For me, the sorrows were ending. I had found Christ (He was never lost, I was), but I found my way back to Him. And for that Methodist couple who led me to Him, I hope there is a huge reward for them in heaven. The abuse was done. I was becoming a teenager, and life was starting to take on a semblance of normalcy. An interesting thing to watch for in this narrative is another Methodist came into my life a few years later, which would entirely alter the course of my life again.

At this point in my story, I am hoping you are starting to see that even though you go through difficulties, trials, abuse, or strange situations, God has never left. He has a design for each of us, and as we progress through each stage, we may not see His hand right away; but in retrospect, we can see He was always there. He said,

> *So do not fear, for I am with you; do not be dismayed, for I am your God. I will strengthen you and help you; I will uphold you with my righteous right hand.* (Isaiah 41:10, NIV)

CHAPTER 3

European Interlude

W hat happens to many folk when they receive Christ happened to me. The abuse had stopped, and I became complacent and more confident in who I was. Dad was still serving in the air force and received a transfer (posting) to Metz, France. At that time, I was getting very proficient in hockey and played with some of the best of those years: Sheldon Kenegeiser, Ian Turnbull, and Bobby Orr. We were all in Little League in the North Bay, Powassan, Trout Creek, and Parry Sound area. We were just kids then. And if I don't mind saying so, I was pretty good. I even received the most valuable player for one year presented by Gordie Howe.

I was good enough that my uncle thought I should stay in Canada and go to St. Michael's School in Toronto. That school was a private preparatory school, and it prepped boys for life and as well for a life of hockey with the Toronto Maple Leafs. My uncle Bob, whom I am named after, suggested to my father that I stay with him in Canada while Dad served overseas in Metz, France. He said he would pay for all my schooling and upkeep and even pay for hockey school and camp. Dad said an emphatic no. He said, "He is my son, and I can look after my own."

I think about that often. I felt that his way of looking after me was more of an inconvenience for him than it was about what I would do or become in life supposedly guided by him. We moved to France, and that ended my hockey days. I never played again until I joined the armed forces myself and played for the air force team. It did not go far. It was not the same as it was when I was a kid, and so I lost interest.

Adventure in Europe

Well, we moved to France, and just after we arrived, President JFK was assassinated, and life changed, not just for me but for everyone. It was unbearable living at home because his drinking was at an all-time high, and he made it sound like the threat of World War III was on our doorstep. I could not stand living there, so I determined I was going to get out of that house and get on my own. God, it seemed, was now on the back burner because everything was seemingly going okay, other than the constant screaming and yelling. But with the physical abuse gone, I guess I felt I didn't need God right then.

I turned seventeen and went to my father and said, "I want to join the air force." He was only too happy to comply. I needed to ask him for permission because you needed your parents' consent to join if you were not eighteen, and Dad couldn't sign the paper fast enough. I guess he figured once I was out of sight, I would be out of mind. Didn't bother me though because it was what I wanted.

I signed. I was sworn in. I left for Canada and basic training one month later.

Me, seventeen years old in the Royal Canadian Air Force

Having completed basic training at the top of my class, I had my choice of postings. Because I had spent much of puberty and my teen years in Europe with no abuse, it had been a new life for me, and I considered France and Germany home and asked to be transferred there. There was a posting in Marseille, France, and that was the one I took. After I arrived, I was only there for a few short months and then transferred to Zweibrücken, Germany. That was okay because my father was still in Germany, but he was stationed a hundred miles away in Baden-Baden in the Black Forest of Germany.

I had completed grade 10, and that was all I needed to get into the forces. But later while in the forces, I returned to school on a plan the air force had for reeducation, and I completed my GED in short order. The problem I had with my newfound independence was, I began to turn into my father. I had a temper that got me thrown in the brig a few times, and I became a drinker and a smoker. The funny thing was, while I was in the brig, God came to my remembrance. I had my little New Testament in my pocket because I carried it even when I was not thinking about God. To me, it was a treasure, and I was not about to lose it even though I was not living the life it demanded. I was allowed to keep it in the jail, which was a blessing. I read it about ten times right through while I was in, and I would pray and memorize scripture, more out of boredom than for spiritual growth.

Then I was out of the brig and back on the job, and everything got back to routine. But now it was coming close to the time that I needed to decide if I would sign on for another three years or not, and I decided, nope, I can make it on my own, and I don't need this military life anymore. It was just a means to an end, getting out of my father's house. So I did not sign for any more time. I was honorably discharged, and because I was in Germany serving, I asked to be released in Germany.

The adventure continued. After being released, I took a job as a civilian on the airbase in Lahr, Germany, which was still fifty miles from where my father was stationed in Baden-Baden. Life was good. I was renting a room in the bunkhouses on the air base, and I was eating in the base cafeteria. I had my own car, and I was single. It didn't get any better—until the unthinkable happened.

My father, like I said earlier, was still in the service, and he was living in Baden-Baden, Germany. I was stationed in Zweibrücken, Germany, and I released from the air force and moved to Lahr, Germany. It was another air force base, only larger and more opportunities. I was working one day when my boss came to me and said, "Hey, Bob, guess who's been transferred here to Lahr from Baden-Baden?" I said, "I don't know," but I was hoping it was one of my friends that had been transferred to Lahr from Zweibrücken because base Zweibrücken was closing. He said, "Your father!" I nearly died on the spot. His job would put him in the building right beside where I was working, and we would share the same cafeteria, and I might even be called on to drive him somewhere. I was working in the MSE section (mobile support equipment), and we supplied rides and/or vehicles to many on the base. I can remember thinking, *God all has been good. Why this? Why now? I am twenty years old, and I am on my own earning a living. I have some money in the bank and a car, and why is this happening?*

Devious Man

Well, Dad showed up, and the first thing he did was step right into my life. He did not say, "What are you doing here?" He said, "Why are you here?" Then the man went off the deep end. I think now, looking back, it might have been that his past with me might come out, and he would lose face or even get in some kind of trouble because of it. So he did something that was so devious I still shake my head today thinking about it.

Canadian law governs Canadians who are living in a foreign country on Canadian Forces bases. Dad knew this. He told me he did not want me in the same place as him and that I should go back to Canada. I told him I am my own person now and that he should just leave me alone. We had been separated for three years, and we should just leave it like that. Well, I did not see him for a couple of days until one morning I showed up for work, and he was there with an MP (military policeman). I think that MP was more for effect than anything else. Anyway, Dad handed me a piece of paper; and when I took it and read it, it was on Department of National Defense stationery. The gist of what was contained in the letter (only because I cannot remember word for word) was that I was declared a dependent of my father, and being such, I was required to live under his roof and do what any dependent does: obey the rules of dependents of service personnel.

Let me explain. Dad had gone to the base legal commander and found out that Canadian law governing dependents of serving personnel in foreign countries were considered the sole responsibility of the parent or guardian until age twenty-one. I was twenty. Dad invoked his right to bring me back home as a dependent. The MP and Dad escorted me to my bunkhouse, collected all my things, and escorted me and my car to my parents' house. After serving in the forces myself for three years now, I was reduced to dependency upon him once again. But his intent was to not keep me at home. He told me that by the end of the week, I would be on a plane back to Canada and out on my ear.

It was early afternoon, and I had lost my job because of the situation. They did not want problems on the base because of the situation. I believe Dad had a hand in me losing my job as well, but I cannot prove it. So Dad went back to work, and I was left at the house to ponder my new life. It took me about five minutes after he was gone to decide what to do. I went outside and got in my car and went back up to the air base and to the bank. I drained my bank account and closed it. Then I went back to his house and took the license plates off my car. It was not worth a whole lot, but it was mine and a little hard to let it go like that. I signed the ownership and put it on the kitchen table. Mom was out somewhere, so it was easy to get away. I packed what I would need in a backpack and took off hiking down the road. I hitchhiked the three hundred miles to Antwerp, Belgium, where I got on a ferry over to England. Once I got to London, I took a job in a strip club shining the lights on the girls and introducing them as the next dancer. I am not proud of that job, but it fed me, and that was all that mattered. I rented a small flat, and life was back to normal, so I thought.

Captured

Can any hide himself in secret places that I shall not see him? saith the LORD. Do not I fill heaven and earth? saith the LORD. (Jeremiah 23:24, KJV)

I thought everything was going good until two months later the strip club closed up. I was out of work, and I could not find any. I hitched to South Hampton, England, where the *Queen Elizabeth 2* was moored. I tried to get a job on her, but they said they were full. Back to London I went. I ended up at the Gatwick Airport, and I was checking into flights back to Germany because I thought I didn't have a choice. At least if I went back there, I could get on a plane to Canada, and I could always go to my grandparents' place. As I was standing at the wicket checking out the cost, I did not realize I was standing next to a small detachment of Canadian airmen. They were checking in to go back to Germany. What I did not realize was the man checking them in was a friend of my father's whom I had met several times. He never said a word, but within minutes, there were two MPs behind me, and I was in handcuffs. There was a warrant out for my arrest, and that they did. I was returned to Lahr, Germany, and when we landed, I was taken to the air force jail where I spent the night. Well, at least the airfare was free. While I was in there, my father came to see me, and all he said was, "You think you are smarter than me. I'll show you."

The next morning, I was escorted to a military plane in hand-cuffs and put on it with my father sitting beside me. The hand-cuffs did not come off until we were in the air. When we landed in Canada, we were met at the airport by my grandfather. He put me in the back seat of the car, and Dad sat in the front. Off we went to Granddad's house. The next morning, my father was gone, and I was free. I would not see my father and mother again for eight years. My grandparents and I never spoke about Dad or Mom and what they had done ever again.

Now begins the next part of the journey that God was taking me on. Amazing as it is to me, I see how God brought me through situations that only He could, most times without me even knowing He was doing it. God said it in His Word:

> *I will instruct you and teach you in the way you*
> *should go; I will counsel you with my loving eye.*
> (Psalm 32:8, NIV)

The next phase of my life is preparation for a mighty encounter with God. Much happens over the next couple of years, but as is the intent of this book, it happens in such a way that it shows no one can doubt that God was putting a plan together, and it will come to fruition. Maybe your life is following a path that you are unsure of. Let me encourage you. God said, "I will perfect the things that concern you, My mercy endures forever. I will not forsake the works of my hands" (Psalms 138:8). Trust Him to work it out. Read the rest of my story and see if you agree with me. God is greater because *"ye are of God, little children, and have overcome them: because greater is He that is in you than He that is in the world"* (1 John 4:4, KJV).

Back in the Homeland

You can well imagine, being free from the mental abuse and oppression from my father was a blessing. I was free and back with people who did not hurt me but spent time with me. My grandparents were the best. They encouraged me, helped me, directed me, and besides all that, housed me and fed me until I got on my feet. They loved me!

Uncle Bob

I was not back in Canada and in my grandparents' house two days, and my uncle Bob showed up. We had a great time reminiscing, and we even discussed Dad for a bit. We talked about how disappointed he was that I was not allowed to stay home from Europe and go to St. Michael's and perhaps on to hockey school. Uncle Bob always had great faith in my hockey abilities, and whenever he could, he had been there to watch me play. Dad never showed at a game or to the hockey banquet when I was awarded MVP for that year and the trophy was given to me by Gordie Howe. But my uncle Bob was there! We had a good relationship.

While he visited with my grandparents and me, he spent the days driving me around to help me get a job. At one time, before making a substantial amount of money in the stock markets and moving to British Columbia, he was the town foreman for Whitby township where I was now. So he got the bright idea to take me down to his old office and speak to the foreman whom he said he knew quite well. He asked him if there was a chance there was some work for me, and the foreman said, as a matter of fact, there was, and that was it. I was working the next day. When I got home from my first day, he was packed and ready to leave for home. He gave me a big hug, told me he loved me, and then grabbed my hand for a handshake. From his hand to mine, he transferred a $100 bill. I had never even seen a hundred-dollar bill in my entire life, let alone own one! He said, "This should keep you until you get your first paycheck." It did!

After he left, the next few weeks fairly flew by what with work and all. But on the weekends, I did not have to ask, and my grandfather would offer me his car. He said, "As long as you gas it and don't drink and drive, it is yours for the weekend." I took care of it, and no, I never took a drink and drove the car. One weekend, he asked me where I was going. Jokingly, I said, "I am going girl hunting." He said, "Can I come?" My grandmother slugged him in the arm! We laughed, and I went out.

Getting My Direction

> *Trust in the Lord with all your heart and lean not on your own understanding; in all your ways submit to him, and he will make your paths straight.*
> (Proverbs 3:5–6, NIV)

REV. DR. ROBERT S.J. COUTTS

Well, the unthinkable happened. The town of Whitby approved a new budget, and it meant cutbacks and layoffs. I was laid off. The next few months, I worked at a steel company, and the same thing happened. I was laid off again. The economy was very sluggish, and jobs were hard to keep, let alone find. I had been looking for jobs in my own neighborhood, so now I needed to expand. My grandfather knew the situation, and he took action. He said, "Get in the car. We are going car shopping." He said it would be easier to travel around to find work. He took me down to the local dealership, and lo and behold, I came home with a turquoise Rambler Classic. As far as I was concerned, it was a dreamboat, probably because it was my own if for no other reason. Hey, it was a Rambler, after all! It was only three years old, and I shone that baby up like nobody's business, put blue lights under the dash, a reverberator (echo chamber) on the radio, and a thrush muffler (backward so it would rumble). This baby rocked, and having the car enabled me to go out of town to look for work, among other things!

God Sent a Wife

"He who finds a wife finds a good thing. And obtains favor from the Lord." Proverbs 18:22, NKJV

Well, it was not long before I found a job seven miles away in Pickering, Ontario. The hydro (Ontario Hydro Electric) was building a nuclear power plant on the edge of Lake Ontario, and they needed hoisting engineers. All I needed was to join the Teamsters Union and pay the dues for the year, and I could start working Monday morning. I did, and I did.

My life was about to become different. I began working at the power plant, and the money was super. Within a couple of months, I had earned enough to trade my Rambler for a two-door, hardtop 1965 Ford Galaxy 500. I checked with my grandfather first because he had bought me the Rambler, and all he said was, "Bob, it's your car. You can do with it what you want. Just make sure you are getting a good deal." Well, the difference in price after trade-in was less than $400, so I took the deal, and it was paid for right away. Another beauty!

Now I had a sporty car (I did some doctoring on this one as well), and I was in seventh heaven. Working at the power plant was a lot of fun, and I became friends with Gordon Brown, a fellow teamster. We hit it off and started hanging around together. We spent our weekends together just hanging out and drag racing down the back roads—illegal but it was a lot of fun.

One particular weekend, we were hanging out at the drive-in restaurant called the Big M in Pickering, Ontario. We were just waiting for some of the other guys to show up and see if they wanted to go out to an old town line road and do some drag racing. It was pretty quiet. That is, until a girl and her friend were walking by the front of the car. In a split second, I was in love with the most beautiful creature I had ever seen. There was such a feeling of warmth and excitement that came all over me that I can't even explain to you what was going on inside. I turned to Gord, and I said, "Gord, do you know who that girl is?" He said, "Yes, that is Daphne Peters." The moment he said her name, I just blurted out—and I now know today that that blurting forth came right out of my heart—"Gord, call her over. I'm going to marry her!" He laughed, but he did not even hesitate. He called her over and introduced her to me. We were kind of shy with each other having just met, but we hit it off instantly.

The next few weeks were a blur. Her birthday was coming, so I got her matching salt and pepper shakers and dishes. She opened the gifts and asked me what I had in mind, and I told her, life together. Then for Christmas, I bought her dishes and an electric steam iron. I have been washing dishes and doing my own ironing ever since, fifty years now!

Well, we had our moments and nearly broke it off once until we both made the decision that we would stay together for good. We moved in together, and as far as we were concerned, we were husband and wife because under Canadian law, we could claim common-law marriage, which gave each spouse the same rights as the marriage license did. We began to make a home for ourselves. (There is way

REV. DR. ROBERT S.J. COUTTS

too much to include here. Suffice it to say, God put Daphne in my path, and I took the bait. It was the biggest right thing I ever did, next to accepting the Lord as my Savior.)

The going was tough for a while, but we managed, and we continued to make our lives with each other work. We spent the next few years living from Vancouver, British Columbia, to the province of Ontario and searching for the right direction for our lives.

The Big Move

The next step in our journey was a particularly hard one but totally led of God. I had been in a raft of jobs, and keeping one for any length of time was a challenge, but really not through any fault of my own. The jobs were as the economy dictated. I finally landed a job at Toronto International Airport as a ramp rat, cleaning and servicing and loading airplanes. The money was not the best, and something was definitely missing. We had moved into the city of Toronto to be closer to the airport, but living in the city was expensive.

I came home from a rather long shift, and all through the shift, I had it in my mind that I needed to head out west where the real work and the real money was. You remember the old saying, "Go west, young man, go west." So when I got home, I sat down with Daphne, and I discussed with her what we should do. Through tears and much discussion, we decided that she and the kids would stay in the apartment in Toronto, and I would head out west in search of better-paying and more stable work. Once found, I would send for her or come and get her.

Both of us having settled it in our hearts, I set out for the west coast of Canada on a quest for a long-term job. Daphne stayed in the apartment and waited for me. To this day, I will never understand that kind of faithfulness to wait and not just throw in the towel and give up on me. I love her more than she knows. We did not know at the time that God was working a plan for our lives. That is what makes it so special to me: His plan and her waiting for me!

Coincidences or Miracles

The sequence of events that happen now cannot be fabricated, and if you recall earlier, when I heard "Bob, everything's going to be all right," then you need to read on because this put the cap on things, as you will see.

Before I go on, I want you to know, I do not believe in coincidences. I believe in miracles. What you will read over the next few pages are about miracles. Indisputable, bona fide, real-life miracles. No one but God could put a story together such as this. My life was totally altered by those miracles, and I will be eternally grateful to my Savior for revealing Himself to me.

> *Jesus said to him, "Because you have seen Me, you have believed; blessed are those who have not seen and yet have believed." Jesus performed many other signs in the presence of His disciples, which are not written in this book. But these are written so that you may believe that Jesus is the Christ, the Son of God, and that by believing you may have life in His name.* (John 20:29–31, NIV)

CHAPTER 4

Work Related

It was early January, winter, and very cold with lots of snow, and I was on my way out to Western Canada in search of the dream job that would support me and my family, I hoped forever. I had left Daphne with enough money to keep her for at least two months. If I did not find work in that time, she would need to apply for welfare; that's government assistance. For me, I had enough to keep me for about three weeks. I hoped to find work before it ran out. My trip was uneventful.

The North Calls

I drove clean out to Vancouver Island and not a job to be found, so I headed back inland and north in British Columbia. I drove until late evening and arrived in Fort St. John on the border of British Columbia and the Yukon Territories. It was a very small town with one store, one restaurant in a hotel, and to my dismay, the hotel was full. No rooms. It meant that I had to sleep in the car, and fortunately, I had nearly a full tank of gas.

It was a long night, and in the morning when I awoke, I went to the restaurant and asked about the possibility of work in or around Fort St John like logging or construction. I was told there was nothing whatsoever. That caused me some disappointment as it was a twelve-hour trip back to "civilization." I went to the gas station and topped up the tank, and two minutes later, I was outside town heading south. This time, though, I took the road that led to Alberta. I did not take the road I came in on from British Columbia.

An Angel?

During the whole trip, I traveled alone and saw many hitchhikers but never picked any of them up. I did not feel it was a particularly safe practice. However, as I headed south, I took note of the temperature, and it was in the minus, like minus twenty degrees! As I was driving, I noticed a young man on the side of the road literally out in the country, outside Fort St. John, hitchhiking. I felt sorry for him and thought, I will pick him up and have some company to keep me awake on the long trip, and he looked safe enough. He got in and was extremely grateful for the ride because it was very cold. He was heading to Edmonton, Alberta, as was I, so I would have company for the whole trip.

We drove till noon and then stopped for a bite to eat. While we were sitting and eating, the conversation turned to why I was traveling. First, it was his turn. He was a European student traveling across Canada and taking odd jobs along the way to support himself. He had been working in the hotel in Fort St. John and had just quit to head out to Edmonton. Why didn't the hotel owner let me have his job that he just quit? The pay was probably minimal anyway and the job was more than likely temporary.

He had been in Canada for a few months already and had started his journey in Vancouver. He said he was gathering information on Canadian culture to include in a thesis he had to do for his final year in college, so that was why he was traveling. Then it was my turn, and of course, I told him my story about my wife and children and so many jobs that just seemed to keep falling apart and also the low pay scales that each one provided. I told him I was following the old adage "Go west, young man, go west," and so here I was.

Then he planted something in my heart that, like I said earlier, changed the direction of my life; although when he told me, I had no clue it was going to do so. He said that when he was in Fort St. John, the hotel manager suggested to him that he should go to the Chamber of Mines in Edmonton if he was looking for permanent work. He was not looking for permanent work but suggested to me that I should at least check it out. I made a mental note to give it a shot after I visited the Manpower Center in Edmonton first.

Well, we finished up lunch and drove into the evening. Edmonton is a big city, and I was not about to drive into it at night not knowing where I was going, so I looked for a motel on the outskirts. My hitchhiker (sorry, I do not even remember his name) said he was going to take a bus into the city and find a youth hostel to stay at. We said goodbye, and he was gone. I wonder to this day if he wasn't an angel sent by God to show me the way. *"Be not forgetful to entertain strangers: for thereby some have entertained angels unawares"* (Hebrews 13:2, KJV). I went to bed because I was tired and the next day was going to be filled with job hunting.

Manpower and Chamber of Mines

God had a definite plan for me because when I woke up and finished breakfast, I asked the motel clerk if he had any idea where the Manpower Center and the Chamber of Mines were. He told me I was in luck. All I needed to do was stay on the road I was on heading into the city, and when I come to Main Street, I was to turn right and go a few blocks. Both the Manpower Center and the Chamber of Mines were right there. He said the Edmonton Hospital was also right across the street. This is also significant as you will see.

I left the motel and drove into the city as I was directed and came to Main Street, turned right, and went three blocks and there both buildings were. I parked in the Manpower Center parking lot because that was going to be my first stop. I went inside and straight to the counter and asked where I could go to see the boards with the jobs. I was directed to another floor, so I went there. When I entered the hall, I saw about twenty-five boards with cards on them listing jobs and contacts. My heart soared. Maybe I just hit the jackpot finally, I thought.

I need to tell you, I was shocked out of my shoes when I went to the first board. Every card on the board listed the Chamber of Mines as the employer but no job on the card. The instructions on the card were to take the card and see the clerk at the check-in at Manpower for instructions. I thought this was a strange thing. So I took a card and went to the counter. The clerk asked me my age, and I told him, "I am twenty-five." He said, "Perfect, how's your health?" I said, "Excellent."

Then he handed me a form and said, "Go across the street and check in at the front desk. They will direct you from there." I asked him what kind of work was it, and he said that they had everything I could think of and that they would evaluate me and let me know if and what they had was suitable for me. Then he said something that made up my mind for me to go over to their building. He said, "I can tell you, you will like the wages!" I took the forms and headed across the street.

The Testing Begins

It was 9:00 a.m., and the building was not overly busy, so I was seen right away. I was taken to a room where a gentleman sat down with me and started asking me questions from what could I do, what have I done, what do I want to do, do I want a permanent job, am I in good health, have I been in trouble with the law, am I an alcoholic, can I drive, was I married, did I have children, and on it went. After that interview, I was given a mind quiz, something like an IQ test that took half an hour to complete, and then sent to a room to wait for the results. About another half hour later, the man came back and said, "We have gone over everything you have provided us, and we would be interested in you working for us if you are interested in working for us. After evaluating you, we have come up with a job we think you can do."

Now, listen to what the man said because later it will tie everything together from my earlier life, and you will see it when I reach my destination. The man asked me, "Can you drive a Euc [that is short for Euclid, although I had no idea at the time]?" I wanted work so bad that I just blurted out without hesitating, "Yup!" He said, "Good, the starting pay is $10.33 per hour." I nearly fainted. That was three times more per hour than any job I had up until now! He said, "But first you need to pass a physical. Take these papers and go across to the hospital, and they will take care of you, and when you are done, come back and see me." All three buildings were across from each other: the Manpower office, the Chamber of Mines, and the Hospital. Go figure, ha-ha!

Physically Fit

I went across to the hospital, and my mind was whirling. I had no clue what a Euc was, and I was afraid to ask in case they said I couldn't have the job because I didn't even know what I was getting into. I am a fast learner, so I figured I could wing it, and the money was enough incentive to find out. I had the physical: blood work, x-rays, and a doctor checked me over thoroughly. I was back in the Chamber of Mines by 2:30 p.m. The results were in. I was physically fine, and they hired me on the spot. I was in such a state of bewilderment that I did not even ask where the job was, when I would start, and I was certainly not going to ask what a Euc was. All I knew was, I was healthy, they wanted me, and they would pay me $10.33 per hour. That's like $30 per hour plus today!

Then it happened. The man asked me if I had transportation. I said I did. He said, "Good, because you have some driving to do. You are going to Pine Point, Northwest Territories, 750 miles straight north to work in a lead and zinc mine." It hit me like a brick to the back of the head. I knew exactly where the Northwest Territories were. The night before, I had just come down from Fort St. John, which is on the territorial line of the Yukon and the Northwest Territories. And now I was heading back! The Northwest Territories are straight north above the sixtieth parallel. I also knew that lead and zinc were usually mined in open pits, not underground, so that part was okay, and I would not need to go underground, which was a good thing. I knew that information because there were mines around North Bay where I spent those abusive years. And the news station on TV carried stories about the mines and what they were producing, so I learned it there. However, at this point, I felt it necessary to explain my situation to the man. I told him I wanted and needed the job. I didn't mind working in the mines, but I only had enough money to support myself for about one more week.

Money from Heaven

God wanted me up there. The man said, "Oh, don't worry, we are going to give you an advance like we do with everyone we hire, and we will take it back off your first month's pay. We will give you enough for three motels, gas, and food and enough to live on until you get your first check. Also you will live in the bunkhouse and eat in the cafeteria, so you won't need much because those are supplied by the mines for the workers. We have sent others up there, so we know the cost. You have three days to get there and report to the security at the mine. If you don't show up, we will inform the RCMP [Royal Canadian Mounted Police], and they will find you [they always get their man], and we will get our money back, and you will be in jail."

Well, I thought, *this is awesome*. It was also too late to leave that evening, so I stayed in the same motel as I did coming into the city because it was the same road I needed to take to head north. I figured, *It is 750 miles, and I can do that in two days and save some money*. I telephoned Daphne, my wife, and we had a nice talk, and I told her the good news and that I thought we would be together again real soon. I left at six o'clock the next morning.

I had the idea I was going to get a job at Manpower and probably end up in another dead end that would require me looking for another job in a few months. The money I started out with in Ontario was almost gone, and I was working my way back toward Ontario and my family before it did run out. I was planning my own way. How foolish. "A man's heart plans his way, but the Lord directs his steps" (Proverbs 16:9). Thank you, Lord, for that direction!

North to a Changed Life

I drove steady and arrived in Pine Point late in the evening of the second day. As I entered the town, I saw the security guard station on the right as I was told it would be and stopped and went in. I introduced myself and gave them my papers. The security guard told me I had to park my car in the security lockup until I received a sticker to place on the windshield signifying I was an employee. I parked it and took my belongings and got in the security truck, and he headed down the road. This is where I want you to be reminded about what I said earlier. The man at the Chamber of Mines had asked me if I could drive a Euc, and I had said yes. But there is more to it than that. Let me go on.

The Shock

I asked the security guard where we were going because it was late in the evening, and the road in front of us and the sky were as black as pitch, and you literally could see nothing. He said we were heading out to the mine location where the bunkhouses were to get me checked in. As we drove along, I noticed that the road was getting rather wide. I mean airplane-runway wide! Then straight ahead of us at the edge of the headlights was a stop sign. Not just any stop sign either. As we got close to it, I jokingly asked the security guard if he could see it because it was no less than twelve feet high. He laughed but said nothing. He said nothing because just as we stopped, I noticed a set of very bright headlights coming from the right. The ground began to shake, and I must admit, I was a bit concerned. Then all of a sudden, the biggest tire I had ever seen in my entire life went by the windshield of the pickup truck we were in. My eyes got huge as I watched this monster wheel go by. I had to lean way forward and look straight up in the air to see what it was attached to. When I saw it, I said to the security guard, "What is that?" He calmly said in reply, "That's a Euc."

150-ton Terex (Euclid, "Euc")

It was fairly dark, and I could not get a real good look at it other than the sheer height of it and the size of the tires, and a man sitting way up in the air! Something leaped in my spirit at that very moment. The look I got of the truck was enough to take me back to my bedroom in North Bay, Ontario, at age eleven. That truck was the very same truck (a replica) of the one in my dream that came up the stairs into my bedroom with Jesus driving and wearing a yellow hard hat. The man in the cab of that truck that just went by also had on a yellow hard hat. You can't make this stuff up! God was bringing the whole plan for my life together. I turned to the security guard with excitement in my voice, and I said with a giggle, "Oh, I am supposed to be driving that thing!" He said, "Aw, there is nothing to it. *Bob everything's is going to be all right.* You get six days training before they turn you loose, and besides, you can steer those things with your baby finger." I laughed and said to him, "That's easy for you to say."

We arrived at the bunkhouse checked in, and I went to bed. I had the biggest smile, and I had tears in my eyes. My Sunday school teachers, Fulton J. Sheen, my grandfather, my uncle, everything came flooding back. I remembered my little New Testament. I had placed it in my suitcase because even though I was not reading it or following the Lord at that time, I still carried it with me. I took it out and looked at it. At that moment, if only for a brief moment, I remembered the Lord, and I said, "Thank You, Jesus!"

The next day, I was checked in and began training. Six days, and I was driving that monster all by myself. I was on cloud nine—well, I was really on twelve-foot tires. I was told my shifts would be seven days' work, three off. Then another seven days' work and three days off. Then it was seven days on and seven off. I was to be paid every fifteen days with nothing held back. Remember, it was 1973, and I was getting $10.33 per hour. That was over $1,000 every pay-day! Also it was possible to send money home to help Daphne and the kids until we could be reunited.

> *But my God shall supply all your need according to his riches in glory by Christ Jesus.* (Philippians 4:19, KJV)

I made a friend on my shift: Louis Michele. He was married and had an infant daughter. He was living in one of the houses provided by the company. The company was called Cominco Mines. Louis owned a small mobile home in the town. There were about 1,800 dwellings in Pine Point, and if you looked at it from the air, all you would see was this long, long line through the bush from the south. It was the dirt roads you drove on to get to Pine Point. At the end of that road was a clearing in the bush. In that clearing was a company made town of prefab houses, mobiles, hotel, bar, restaurant, arena, post office, medical center school, and a bank. The mobile home Louis owned was up for sale.

Town of Pine Point, Northwest Territories

It was one-and-a-half bedrooms, and it was 10' × 35'. It also had a 10' × 12' add-on. Louis wanted $4,500. And he agreed to sell it to me for a small down payment and a few dollars a payday until it was paid. It was fully furnished, and the furnace worked. It needed a little work, but it was our future home. I called Daphne and told her that I bought a small fixer-upper.

I went to my boss and asked about the assistance they were offering to transport families up to the mines. To my surprise, they paid for the whole thing and told me I could have a week off to go out to Edmonton to pick Daphne and the kids up at the airport. The whole trip for her to fly from Toronto to Edmonton, and me to go and get her was on the company. Once again, God was showing us he was working on our behalf. Unfortunately, I was not giving in to serving Him. I was more concerned with making a life and having the family back together.

I retrieved my family and brought them to Pine Point. Daphne was not really impressed with my choice of living accommodations when she got there. It was 10' × 35' and a 10' × 12' add-on. We five were packed in there like sardines. The trailer had such a small washroom that when you walked up to it, you needed to turn around and back into it. When we had a bath, we had to put heaters in the room all day to melt the ice off the walls around the tub so we would not freeze. We ate in different locations in the trailer because it was a two-person kitchen. But we were together, and Daphne faithfully stood by me. I worked hard and even took double shifts for the extra money so we could save up and buy a bigger and better place.

Medical Interruption

All was going well until September of the year we arrived. I was driving out of one of the open pits in my "Euc" when the next thing I knew, I was off the road, and I had passed out. When I awoke, the foreman was beside me, and there was blood everywhere.

I was taken to the medical center in town where there were only two nurses who came to town twice a week. They said I needed to go to Hay River, a town sixty miles west of Pine Point. It was the hub of the north where roads divided and went off into the wilderness to Indian reservations, and it was also the barge port on Great Slave Lake, where barges went farther north.

There was a hospital in Hay River owned and operated by the Pentecostal Assemblies of Canada (I did not know this information then). There was no ambulance service, so the nurses asked me if I felt well enough to drive. I did, and I took off after telling my wife what was going on. It was a sixty-mile drive, and they knew I was coming. When I got to the hospital, I started bringing up more blood, so they rushed me into the ER and put a tube down my throat into my stomach and began pumping cold water into me to stop the bleeding. It seems they knew before I got there what the problem was, and just to verify, they took x-rays and found that I had two burst ulcers: one peptic, the other duodenal. They stopped the bleeding, and later that night, the doctor (Dr. Earl Covert) came in and said, "Take a look at these x-rays." He showed me the duodenal ulcer and how it had burst and left an opening in my intestines. The peptic ulcer was just as bad. He said, "It is a wonder you did not die. We will look at it again in the morning and decide what to do." Then he said something that blew me away: "Don't worry, son. We will be praying for you." I thought to myself, *I hope you know what you are doing, and you are not just going to pray.*

Mrs. Margret Chance

A little later, a nurse came into the room. She was a Methodist nurse working in the Pentecostal hospital. Do you remember I told you to watch for this when I gave my life to the Lord in that Sunday school with the Methodist couple? Well, she (Margaret Chance) came into the room, and all she had in her hands was a Bible. She said, "Mr. Coutts, would you like a devotion?" Even though I had been to Sunday school, I did not know what a devotion was. It was a term I had never heard before, so I said to her, "Sure." I actually thought I was going to get something substantial to eat. In a way, unbeknownst to me, I really was getting something to eat: the Bread of Life. Well, Margaret read from the Bible, and then she said, "Can I pray with you?" It all started to flood back from my childhood. I did not say anything about being saved when I was younger. Instead I let her pray. When she did, I felt something I had not felt before. It was like a warm tingling all over. She prayed and asked God to touch my body and to lead me to a saving knowledge of Jesus (she did not know I had done that as a child); then she left. Before she left, she said, "I will see you tomorrow."

The next day was a battery of tests and more x-rays with no decision. I was not feeling too bad, but I was sure hungry. They had me on a bland white diet, yuck. That evening, Margaret came back as promised; and when she came into the room, I felt that tingling again even before she spoke. The guy in the next bed to me whispered to me to be careful because, as he put it, "they will cram that stuff down your throat." Well, Margaret did exactly as she had the night before; and as she was leaving, said she would be back the next day.

A Miracle

The next morning, Dr. Covert came in about 10:00 a.m., and the first words out of his mouth were, "Look at this." I asked what I was looking at, and he said, "It's the x-rays we took yesterday. And this set are the ones of when you came in." I looked at them, and where the hole was yesterday was completely gone today. He said, "Son, you were healed! You can go home today. Your intestines are intact, and God has healed you." I did not know anything about healing because at the young age I was saved, I was not taught those things. I was told stories like David and Goliath, and Jonah and the whale, and the Red Sea. But nothing about healing. I was not sure what to say or do, so I just said thank-you, packed up, and went back to Pine Point and tried to explain to Daphne what was told to me. Neither one of us understood, but a chain of events followed that would eventually explain everything.

CHAPTER 5

Set Apart by God

The Preacher

After my little stint in the hospital, things pretty much returned to normal. About a week after I was released from the hospital, Daphne and I had a visit from a preacher. He was a Pentecostal minister who had just moved to town. His name was Reverend Ritchie Hayward. Now, I want you to know that I believe God has a sense of humor. I did not think about that, nor did that thought enter my mind when the preacher came knocking. But looking back, I can see it for sure. I say that because, first, I end up in a Pentecostal hospital. Second, I get Pentecostal doctors. Third, a Methodist nurse reads the Bible to me and gives me devotions; and fourth, a Pentecostal preacher knocks on my door, and he tells us that he is new in town, and they have started building a church in the community. And here is where I believe God's sense of humor—or maybe a better way to describe it is *divine plan*—comes in. The preacher told Daphne and I where he lived. He lived in the mobile home directly behind ours. He said they would be moving soon into the new church parsonage, which was attached to the new church building. Why would God put that preacher in a mobile home behind us? Well, He is God, and He had a plan for us, just like I have been telling you all along.

The reason God put that preacher in a mobile directly behind ours was because Reverend Hayward had kids as well as us, and being so close together, they became friends and played together. God used the Haywards' kids to get our attention. His kids asked our kids if they wanted to go to Sunday school. So the preacher showed up at our door and asked if our kids could go to Sunday school with his kids, and he would pick them up in the church van. We thought this was a good idea because I remembered going as a kid myself and loving it. We agreed, and that Sunday, right on schedule, he came and picked them up. Daphne and I thought this was great. We could sleep in a bit while the kids were at the church.

Reverend Hayward came faithfully on Sundays and picked up our kids without fail, and life went on. As the kids got grounded in the Sunday school, they met more children; and as they met more children, we met more parents. Those parents were very friendly, and they invited us for suppers and weekend picnics.

Christmas was approaching, and we received an invitation to the church for their Christmas dinner. We thought we would go just to check it out. When we arrived for the dinner, the tables were all set up and decorated for Christmas, and we had a wonderful time. Daphne and I would slip outside for a quick cigarette and then back inside for more fun. What we did not know until months later was that the church people had all been warned to not say a word to Daphne and me about our smoking, and they were faithful and did not.

Well, after the banquet, we started spending more time with the people because they were really nice, and they seemed honest, and as well, everyone had kids. They never pushed their religion on us, but they did talk about things they had heard that Sunday in church or Wednesday in Bible study. Still we did not go to the church services.

A Cup of Sugar

In late March of 1975, Daphne and I were at home, and it was about 1 p.m., and there was a knock at the door. It was one of the ladies from the church, Margret Chretien. She said, "I am baking my husband an apple pie for supper, and I ran out of sugar. Could I borrow a cup?" We said sure, and she came in. While Daphne was digging out the sugar, I turned to Margret and said, "Margret, something has been bothering me all week. When we were talking on Monday, you had told us something you heard in church on Sunday about the

Second Coming of Christ. I don't know much about the Bible other than what I learned about the main stories kids get taught. What does it mean, second coming?"

I guess that was all Margret needed, although we did not know it at the time. For the next four hours, Margret took Daphne and me on a ride through the book of Revelation that blew my mind. When she was done, she said, "You should come to church on Sunday because Pastor Hayward is speaking on that topic again, the Second Coming of Christ." We said we would think about it. Well, Margret left, and she did not even take the sugar. She said, "It's too late to make the pie for Louis tonight. I'll shop tomorrow and get some sugar then." She left with a smile, and I, for one, was left with a mind that was spinning.

> *But in your hearts honor Christ the Lord as holy,*
> *always being prepared to make a defense to anyone*
> *who asks you for a reason for the hope that is in you;*
> *yet do it with gentleness and respect.* (1 Peter 3:15,
> ESV)

Margret did just that!

For the next few days at work and at home, all I could think about was the things Margret had shared. Saturday came, and I said to Daphne, "Let's go to church tomorrow and see what this is all about." Daphne said, "You go, and you tell me when you get home." That night, I did not sleep good. I was wondering what to expect when I got to the church. I was up early, and away I went; and when I got there, I received so many "we are so happy you cames." It was overwhelming because they were so sincere and nice, and I really did feel welcome.

A Reminder

Before I go on, I want to remind you about having been in the Pentecostal hospital with bleeding ulcers. And I want to remind you about the prayer the doctor prayed for healing and the Methodist

60

nurse Margret Chance who gave me a devotion and prayed for my salvation. Have you got that? Good because this is special.

The First Service

The service started, and Reverend Ritchie Hayward began to preach. For the next forty-five minutes, he tied together everything Margret had told Daphne and me a couple of days earlier. When he was finished preaching, we sang a worship song; and during that song, I felt the same tingling I had felt in the hospital when Margret Chance had prayed for me. As soon as the song was done, something happened that I had never heard or experienced in my life. Someone in the congregation began to speak very loud. The problem was, it was in what I thought was a foreign language, and I did not recognize it. Then another person began to speak very loudly after the first one. This one was in English, and the words were like a repeat of some of the sermon. But at the end of it, the person said, "I am the Lord, and I am speaking to you. If you hear me in your heart, come unto me now." I was sitting with someone I knew, and I turned and whispered to him, "What was that all about?" He said, "That was God speaking through His people and delivering us a message." Then he said, "Maybe He is speaking to you!"

The Call

> *Fight the good fight of faith; take hold of the eternal life to which you were called, and you made the good confession in the presence of many witnesses.* (1 Timothy 6:12, ESV)

At that moment, Reverend Hayward began to speak again. He said, "If you are here this morning and you are not ready for heaven, you need to renounce your sin and accept Christ as your Savior and invite Him to take up residence in your heart because He is coming soon, and He wants us all to be ready. If that is you, please slip up your hand so I can pray for you."

My Salvation

Flashback! At age eleven in North Bay, Ontario, a Methodist couple said the sinner's prayer with me, and I accepted the Lord. I was probably too young to completely understand the action I took that day, although God knew what I did. This couple had told me, "Bob, everything is going to be all right." That may have influenced my decision, but I did make the decision.

Now here I was, sitting in a church with the offer of salvation before me. This time, I understood what was going on. These thoughts flashed before me quickly, and I needed no more time. I slipped my hand up and accepted Christ. Then the preacher invited any who had raised their hand to come forward so he could pray the sinner's prayer with us. I stood and turned to step out into the aisle. As I did, I was confronted with the shock of shocks. Sitting across the church in another pew was Nurse Margret Chance. She was staring at me and smiling and weeping at the same time. I had not seen her for nearly a year, and here she was, sitting in the same church on the day I gave my heart to Jesus. I went forward and was prayed for. I said the sinner's prayer and became a child of God that day, this time with the full knowledge of what I had just done. After the service, I sought out Margret, and we hugged, and all I could think of to say was, "Margret, thank you!" I went home and told Daphne what I had done. She knew I had done something because my whole demeanor and attitude was different, and she said so.

Daphne's Salvation

The next day, we had a visit from the pastor, and he talked to us about what I had done and what it meant. Then he invited us to Bible study on Wednesday. He said, "It will help you to grow in the

Lord by studying His Word." We said we would talk it over. Daphne and I did just that, and she decided she would go if a friend of hers would go with her. She said she would like to know more about the Bible if nothing else. Her friend agreed to go, and we all showed up at the study. There were not a lot of people there, but we knew most of them. The study was real interesting, and things were making sense. Then the pastor asked Daphne if she wanted to accept the Lord as her Savior. Having been brought up Catholic, all she really knew was the Catholic way, although she never practiced it. The priests had told her that you cannot read the Bible for yourself and try to interpret it. Leave it up to the priests. This was completely new to her, so for about half an hour, Pastor Ritchie explained to Daphne what it was about and how and why to do it. Finally, Daphne said, "All right, if you think I need to do it, I will." Then she said the sinner's prayer and accepted Jesus into her heart. She was eternally saved that evening and a changed person. God washed her of her sins and gave her a new life with a guarantee of heaven. God brought our family into the kingdom that day.

> *For by grace are ye saved through faith; and that not of yourselves: it is the gift of God: Not of works, lest any man should boast.* (Ephesians 2:8–9, KJV)

Daphne and I both received the gift of God, and it was not done by any power of our own. It was a work of the Holy Spirit.

Growing in the Lord

The next year was a time of growing in the Lord. The church gave each of us a Bible. It was called the Way, and it was in modern English and easy to understand. Right away, we both began to have devotions. The first book of the Bible we would study was the book of Job. Little did we know how pertinent that would be to us later in life. Watch for the connection a little later.

We fellowshipped on a regular basis with our new family of Christian friends. We went on snowmobile rides, church picnics, fishing, church specials, and we found ourselves spending many evenings at church people's homes. We were a close-knit group, and when we would get together, the conversation invariably turned to the things of God. These were lasting friendships we built and stayed in touch for many, many years. Sadly, some have gone on to be with the Lord, but the memories of them and Pine Point, Northwest Territories, are still fresh to us. We grew fast, and shortly after accepting Christ, Daphne and I went through the waters of baptism, signifying to everyone that we were sold out to God.

A New Home

Well, we were still living in the small trailer, and it was mighty tight. Small and very cold in the winter. I was on a seven-day-off cycle, and I told Daphne I was going fishing for the day. I hadn't done much fishing for a while, and this was a good opportunity, I told her. However, that was not my real intent. What I was really going to do first was drive to Hay River (where the Pentecostal hospital is) and look at new mobile homes. I had applied for a trailer lot from the company first to make sure I had a new lot to put the new mobile on—if I got the new mobile, that is. The lot was approved, and as well, it was in the new part of the town. Also, I had been to the bank and was approved for a loan to buy a new mobile, and I was going to use the one we lived in as a trade-in.

I went to Hay River, and it was easy! I settled on a fourteen-feet-by-seventy-two-feet fully furnished, brand-spanking new mobile home. I was done and back in Pine Point by 2:00 p.m., so I went fishing. And I actually caught some great northern pike. So when I went home, there were no questions, and I could keep it a secret until the delivery date, which was in two days. Well, those two days could not go fast enough. I wanted desperately to spill the beans, and it was so hard to keep quiet, but I did. I had been told they would deliver it at 10:00 a.m., so when 10:00 a.m. came around, I said to Daphne and the kids, "Get in the car please. I have a surprise to show you." Of course, there were questions, but I insisted they wait until the surprise showed up.

We drove out to the entrance to our town where we could see a few miles down the road. The roads in the Northwest Territories at that time were all dirt, and it was summer—hot, dry, and very dusty. Well, we were not there five minutes, and I could see a cloud of dust coming down the road. As it got closer, I knew it was the trailer. At that moment, I said to Daphne, "I bought us a new mobile home, and that's it coming down the road." Well, she refused to believe me. I said, "I am supposed to meet them here, and they will follow me to the new site where our home will be placed on blocks." She still did not believe me. Long story short, the truck towing the mobile followed me to our new site, and when we arrived, we all got out of our vehicles, and the truck driver came over to us and said, "Are you Mr. Coutts?" At that moment, my family believed me, and there was a lot of smiles and yelling with joy. They installed the trailer, we signed the delivery sheet, and went inside, and you would have thought we had died and gone to heaven. There was so much room. Everything was so big. It was full of new furniture, and it was ours. God had truly blessed us. He saved our souls and then began pouring into them. What a Savior.

We moved in two days later because we needed to get electricity and an oil tank hooked up, as well as settle up with the mine administration office. It was only $20 month lot fees, and they told us they would give us all the boards and nails for a fence and cement for a patio and driveway, grass seed, and anything else required to make it look good. It was their property, and because their employees were living on it, the company wanted the lots to look nice. About a week later, our old trailer was resold. I hope the person who moved into it had the same great experiences we had, including salvation.

A Sister in Crisis

We settled in our new home, and by now I was on the church board and teaching a boys' Sunday school class. Eight-year-olds.

What a blast that was. We were enjoying our time. Then one evening, I received a call from my sixteen-year-old sister Mary. She was living at home with our parents in Comox, British Columbia. She was still under Dad's roof, and although she never told me everything, her time there was just as trying as when I was home. She asked me—rather, begged me—to come and get her. She wanted to come and live with us. Mary and I had always been close. I had practically raised her when she was little. I would change her diaper, rock her to sleep, make her formula—all this when Mom was sick in the hospital and Dad was drunk. So I discussed it with Daphne, and we agreed to take her in. It was a two-day drive to British Columbia, and I had to go by myself because we had three children, and it would have been too difficult. So on my next seven-day-off cycle, I went.

I went to Comox, and when I pulled into the driveway, it was in fear and trepidation. I had not seen my parents in eight years, and I did not know what to expect. They did not know I was coming because I had made Mary promise to not tell them so it would save any more abuse to her and problems about me coming.

I got out of the car and went up to the door. I did not have to knock because Mary was already at the door. She hugged me and began to cry. At that very moment, my father came barging out of the house right past me and hollered at my mother, "I'm going to the f—— legion. I don't need this s—— or him!" (pointing to me on the way out). And he was in his car and gone. Mary asked me to come into her room and get her suitcase because it was too heavy for her. As I stepped into the house, my mother was sitting on a chair with my three other sisters. She stood up and looked me in the eye and said, "I don't know you! You are not my son!" And then she left the room.

It all happened so fast that I did not have a chance to say one word. So I picked up Mary's suitcase and put it in the car, and we left. I was totally bewildered by my mother's comment and not sure how to react, so we just left. The journey home was filled with Mary unloading all the stuff that transpired at home. I knew she needed to vent to clear her mind, so I just let her talk, and I listened. It is not part of this story, so suffice it to say, we drove back to Pine Point, Northwest Territories, and we arrived in two days.

A Solemn Greeting

It was early afternoon when we arrived back in Pine Point. As I pulled into our driveway, the next-door neighbor came running from her house and came to the side of the car before I even got out. I rolled down the window, and she blurted out, "Oh, Bob, your wife had to rush your son to Hay River hospital because he fell out of the car while it was moving and broke his arm." Well, you can imagine how I felt at that moment. I had come past Hay River almost an hour ago, and if we had cell phones back then (I don't think they were even invented yet), I could have heard from my wife and stopped at the hospital. Well, Mary and I did not even get out of the car. I just turned around and went back to Hay River and to the hospital.

Once inside, I located my wife, who was sitting in a waiting room. First, we greeted, and right away I asked her what happened and how did he fall out of the car? She was quite surprised and said, "He didn't fall out of any car, and I don't know where our neighbor got her information." Then she explained he looked fine physically, but a day after I had left to get Mary, she noticed that he had many lumps on his neck and under his arms. She had taken him to the clinic in Pine Point, thinking he had mumps. She said she waited in the clinic for about three hours before the nurses came out and told her that they needed to take Bobby to the hospital in Hay River. They took him and Daphne by car. She had left our girls at a friend's house. That was why she was still waiting. She said he wasn't sick or anything, but he had a lot of lumps.

Well, we waited about another hour, and finally the doctor came out and told us the tests were nonconclusive and that he needed to go to the hospital in Edmonton for in-depth treatment to find out what it was. They said they would make all the arrangements to get him to the Charles Camsell Veterans Hospital, which was also a cancer hospital. They said it would be one week before everything was ready for him to go. We took Bobby home, and he was not acting sick, but the lumps were increasing in number and size. That was a Friday. On Sunday, we went to church and took Bobby to the altar and asked the pastor to anoint him with oil and pray for him. He did.

One week later, Daphne and Bobby flew to Edmonton, and he was admitted and began a number of tests. Daphne was with him for five days, and I asked the company for time off, and I drove out to Edmonton to be with them. A friend stayed with Mary and our kids while we were gone. We stayed in Edmonton for two more days while the doctors tested Bobby. Then they came to us with the final diagnosis. Their words to us were like a knife cutting us. "We are sorry to tell you, but it is non-Hodgkin's lymphoma, and he has about 150 swollen lymph nodes. We think you should prepare yourselves because he is not going to make it. He probably has just over a week to live." Even though he was not exhibiting a sickness, the cancer was eating him quickly.

We were stunned, but right away, we got hold of the pastor, and we told him what the doctors had said, and the whole church began to pray while we were with our son, and Pastor said he was coming to Edmonton as well and would come by the hospital and pray with him. The news the doctors had given us was not what we wanted to hear.

However, what I am going to tell you now is an actual miracle that happened before our very eyes, as well as the doctors and nurses and our pastor who had come to Edmonton and was at the hospital that day with us. You remember I told you earlier, I do not believe in coincidences. I believe in miracles!

Divine Intervention

Here is what happened. Daphne and I had taken Bobby to the altar before coming to the hospital, and we turned him over to God. We had prayed over him. We were new Christians, and we just believed God. We had been studying the book of Job, of all things, and now we were in the test. Now here we are faced with losing him, and Daphne and I were at peace. In that room where our son lay that day were nurses, doctors, Daphne and I, and our pastor. We asked everyone if they minded if we prayed before they left. Everyone agreed, and so Pastor Hayward prayed over Bobby and asked God to heal him but to have his way with him. Also in that prayer, we said, "Lord, he is Your child. We trust you to do Your will. If You want to take him home to Yourself, we give him to You, and we will continue to serve You. We would rather You let us keep him and raise him, but nevertheless, let Your will come to pass."

At that very moment, lymph nodes started shrinking until every one of them was no longer visible. A nurse started crying. One doctor said we needed to do some more tests. But we knew in our hearts what had just happened. They kept our son in for a few more days doing test after test and always coming up with the same answer. There was no trace of the disease. They released him, and we went back to Pine Point. The doctors recorded his healing in their records in the Charles Camsell Hospital in Edmonton, Alberta, as "divine intervention." How could they call it anything else? To this day in the Charles Camsell Veterans Hospital in Edmonton, Alberta, Canada, the words "divine intervention" are recorded in their records. To God be the glory. As of this writing, our son is forty-five years of age and not a trace of the disease. PTL!

CHAPTER 6

The Call

After we returned to Pine Point, things began to settle down again. Our faith had been tested, and God was faithful. Our boy was alive and healed, and our faith was strengthened further. We spent the next few months fellowshipping with the people of the church and enjoying one another's company. Mary, my sister, got involved in the church youth group, and not long after that, she accepted the Lord as her Savior. She did not stay with us long. About ten months and then she made arraignments with a good friend back in Comox, British Columbia, to live with her. We made sure she was able to get there safely, and she left. Her life changed after that. It was not long, and she met a young man and married him. But her story is her own, and she should tell it. We did what we had to do to help, and that was the end of it.

The fall was coming, and so was the men's fellowship retreat. It was to be held in Banff Springs, Alberta, over a four-day weekend. Pastor asked if I would like to go, and having never been to anything like it before, I was unsure what I was getting into. However, I said I would go. He asked me to be prepared to give my account, a testimony, of what transpired at the meeting. He said it would encourage others if I did. Little did I know what it would do to me or for me, but I agreed. There were five men from our church going, and we loaded up in the church van, and away we went to the retreat. It was a long drive, but it turned out to be fun—that is, when we were not sleeping and taking turns driving. It was a nine-hundred-mile drive that took eighteen hours nonstop except for pit stops.

When we arrived, I was overwhelmed by the beauty of the place. A majestic hotel nestled in the Rocky Mountains. Snow all around and covering the mountains made it a beautiful spectacle, and it was

God who created it. The inside of the hotel was unlike any I had ever seen, or been in for that matter. It looked expensive is probably the only way I can describe it. Just inside the main doors, there was an opening under the wall and a large pool in front of the wall. There were steps leading into the pool, and I saw people in bathing suits walking down those steps and then under the wall to an outside pool. The clerk explained that it was the hot springs, and it was natural water coming from the ground at an average temperature of eighty-one degrees Fahrenheit. It was about minus twenty degrees outside, so we were all looking forward to the hot springs.

Banff Springs Hotel

The hot springs

Called to Ministry

We settled in for the evening and decided we would try out the hot springs. We all changed and headed for the pool. The others all went straight out into the pool. They knew what they were doing because they had been here the year before. I was the new kid on the block and probably a little nervous or more intimidated by the collection of nothing but men in the pool, so I stood just under the wall on the outside of the building. The hot spring was fantastic. Freezing outside and eighty-one degrees in the water. I was getting a little tired in the legs from just standing in the water, and there were benches all around the side of the pool in the water to sit on. So I searched out a spot where I thought I would be less intimidated. I spotted an opening over to one side of the hot springs between a post and an elderly gentleman. I thought that looked safe enough, so I went over and sat down on the bench in the water. It was awesome. The water came up to my chin, and I was in heaven. I sat there quietly for a few minutes, and then out of the blue, the older gentleman that was beside me turned and looked right in my eyes. If they could have burned a hole, they would have. He said, "What is your name, son?" I said, "Bob, sir." Then still staring right into my eyes, he said, "I do believe God is going to make you a preacher, son." I said nothing because I was stunned and did not know what to say. He never said another word to me; he just left the pool. I kept that to myself because I was not sure what to make of it.

The next morning after breakfast, we went to the first meeting of the day. The speaker for the weekend was the general superintendent of the Pentecostal Assemblies, and it was none other than the elderly gentleman I had sat beside in the pool the night before, Reverend Robert Argue. He spoke, and I will tell you, I have never heard more powerful speaking than I did from that man over the next few days. The men's fellowship retreat was over all too soon. The superintendent's words were burning in my heart, and I started to feel that the message he gave me was true because of the content of the messages over the days we were there, and as well, all I could think about was that I should be a preacher. But when or how and even why? We headed home.

First Pulpit Experience

When we arrived home, things were different for me. I told my wife what had happened and how I could only think about those words and that I was not really sure what to do. We went to church on Sunday, and the pastor invited me to the pulpit to give an account of what happened at the retreat. I never gave it a thought until I reached the pulpit and turned around and saw all those people sitting there staring at me. It was the funniest thing you ever saw. My mind turned to jelly, and my voice shook so bad that you would think I was a walking earthquake. I started out talking to the people about what transpired, and by the time I was done, I was ducked down behind my arm leaning on the pulpit. The pastor came up to me when I was finished and said, "Good job, Bob. Thanks for that report." To this day, neither I nor Daphne can tell you one word of what I said. All I remember thinking was, *I will never go up to a pulpit like that again, ever!* Think again Bob.

> *"For I know the plans I have for you," declares the Lord, "plans to prosper you and not to harm you, plans to give you hope and a future. Then you will call on me and come and pray to me, and I will listen to you. You will seek me and find me when you seek me with all your heart."* (Jeremiah 29:11–13, NIV)

Nicknamed Preacher

Now that the testimony was out of the way, we continued on with church life. I had earned the nickname of preacher at work, and that was a funny story in and of itself, but it just confirmed the general superintendent's words in my life. You see, like I have been telling you throughout this whole story, God knows what we need and when we need it. He said He will guide us, and He means it. If you are in need of direction, His Word will provide you each step, and

His Holy Spirit will make it come alive in you. So just keep looking to Him. *Everything's going to be all right.*

Back to the nickname *preacher.* I had graduated from driving Euclid trucks to becoming a blasthole driller. It was a job I loved, and the wages were substantially more. The hours were longer though. I would work twelve-hour days for seven days at a time. But with the money we were making, we were getting further ahead all the time. Daphne had been taken on at the school in town as an assistant teacher and making a real good wage as well. We were doing well.

I received the nickname *preacher* when one day I was traveling out to the open pits to get on my drill. We were transported out to the pits in what was called a crummy. A crummy was nothing more than a crew cab truck, and it took six of us at a time, including the driver and all our gear in the truck box. The day I received my nickname, I was sitting in the back seat between two huge men. I weighed 147 pounds, and these guys were about 275 each. There were three more in the front that were the same size. They were all great guys, and we got along. But this one day we were headed out to the pit, and the guys were laughing and joking; and because they were unsaved as a flock of geese, they didn't mind using off-color language. Usually I would just shut it out of my mind, but this trip was different.

They were cursing up a storm, and all at once, the driver took the name of Jesus in vain. Out of nowhere, I must have had enough because out of my mouth burst these words, "He's the Savior of my soul." Well, you could have heard a pin drop. It went dead silent in the truck for the next few minutes. We had about a half-hour drive, and we were only halfway. I was thinking to myself, *I have done it now. They are going to beat me up, or worse, tar and feather me.* Well, about five minutes went by, and they started talking and joking again. It wasn't long before the cursing started again, and then one of the other guys took the Lord's name in vain again. It must have been a reflex (I found out later it was the Holy Spirit), but out it came again: "He can save your souls as well." Well, now I had done it. So I thought! It was absolutely quiet until we reached the pit. Everyone went their own way without saying another word. When the shift was over, they all came in the truck, and I was the last to be picked up. All the way back to the mine site, the conversation was clean and not one curse word. As a matter of fact, when I was in the truck, these guys became the most polite guys on the planet. When they picked me up the next morning for our shift and we got in the truck, this is how they addressed me: "Good morning, preacher," "How ya doing, preach?" "Great day today, huh, preacher?" And so it was. I was called *preacher* or *preach* from then on.

Now here is the rest of that story. Over the next few months, I had many chances to witness to some of those men, and three of them received Christ as Savior and started attending the church. The other two actually moved away, so I don't know what happened to them. But from that moment on, it seemed to me they began to respect the Lord that was in me and never took His name in vain in front of me again.

I kept attending and being involved in the church, and by now everything I was reading and hearing was leading me to believe that God was calling me into ministry. We had been in Pine Point since 1974, and now it was 1977 and early February. I was so convinced by now that God wanted me in ministry, and I had many good talks with Daphne about it but still was unable to decide what to do until we were visiting a friend's house one night. He was a supervisor at the mine. We were talking about rumors we had heard about the mine closing. There seemed to be some uncertainty among a lot of the people. As we were talking, Trevor, the man we were visiting, said, "I have some news. We are moving to Fort McMurray. The company, Syncrude, is hiring like crazy, and they need every trade available." We asked when he was going, and he said it would be in the fall if our company didn't shut down first according to the rumors.

At that moment, something in me made a decision. We went home, and I said to Daphne that we needed to tell our pastor that God had called me to ministry, and we needed direction. We agreed, and the next day, we went to him and told him what was on our minds. All he said was, "Nope, God is not calling you. That's just your imagination." I felt a bit deflated, but still I went home with Daphne, and I said to her, "We need to find out from God if He really is calling me or not." She agreed, and we came up with a plan.

At that time, there were no mobiles for sale, and no one was buying anything anyway because of the uncertainty they felt. So I said to Daphne, "This is what we are going to do. If it happens, we will take that as a sign from God to head to Bible college." What we would do was we would go down to the post office and put a sign up saying we had a trailer for sale. If it sold within one week, we would know we were supposed to go. If not, we would forget about it. So he made a sign, and I went down to the post office to post it where everything in the town that was for sale was posted. There were a few people in the post office, but no one that I knew. I put the sign up and drove home.

When I arrived back at the house, there was a man and woman standing on our step. I got out of the car and greeted them. They said they were in the post office when I put the sign up, and they saw the address and drove here to meet with me. I was a little taken aback because that was like ten minutes earlier. So I said, "Come in and have a look."

My wife met us inside, and she took the man's wife to the back of the trailer to see it. The man walked into the living room with me and took a quick look around and said, "How much you asking?" I was not even prepared. I had not discussed it with my wife, and I was not sure what the market would bear, especially given the working climate in the town right now. But out of nowhere, I blurted out, "I want $18,500. We had paid $14,900 for it and lived in it almost two years." The man never even took a breath. He said, "Sold," and stuck out his hand for a handshake to seal the deal. I was flabbergasted. His wife and mine came down the hall, and he said to her, "Honey, it's ours." We agreed to go to the bank the next day and settle up the finances and set a date to take over. After they left, my wife and I just looked at each other and laughed. Never mind it selling in one week, how about just ten minutes! Now we had to tell our pastor!

A Negative

Well, telling our pastor did not go well. He was totally convinced that I was not called to go into ministry and did everything he could to change our minds. We dearly love Pastor Hayward, but when it came to the call of God on my life, it was not up to him, and I let him know it. (Watch for some irony in his feelings a little later in this work. It's funny!)

We never gave in. It was at that point that I knew, that I knew, that I knew! We had settled on the first of June as our date to leave. Reluctantly, Pastor Hayward helped put together a farewell dinner at the church for us. It was tough leaving those people because we were all a family, and we were close. God had brought us all the way to the Northwest Territories to save us and call us into ministry and make many, many friends in the process. He grounded us in the Word and performed miracles in our lives. Now we were about to embark on a new adventure, and do you know what? We knew *everything's going to be all right!*

At first, many of the men in the church tried to convince us to go to Fort McMurray, Alberta. Many of them were thinking about going themselves, and some were already preparing to go. The work was just starting in McMurray, and the wages were almost double what we were getting in Pine Point. The rumors of Pine Point either shutting down or laying off were playing havoc with the townspeople. We have to admit, we were tempted to follow the money, but the call of God was way stronger.

We had our minds made up, and we needed to get ready to go. The car we had we felt would not make it, so we spoke to a man in the church that had a 1969 Ford for sale and a hardtop tent trailer. After securing both of these items, we proceeded to get ready. The day arrived for us to leave. We said our goodbyes and had prayer then took off.

An Unforgettable Journey

The following account is a trip Daphne and I would love to forget. But it is worth telling because it goes to show how hard the devil works against you when you are sold out and following the Lord.

77

But it also shows how God is with us every step of the way and how everything will be all right.

> *Put on the whole armor of God, that ye may be able to stand against the wiles of the devil. For we wrestle not against flesh and blood, but against principalities, against powers, against the rulers of the darkness of this world, against spiritual wickedness in high places. Wherefore take unto you the whole armor of God, that ye may be able to withstand in the evil day, and having done all, to stand.*
> (Ephesians 6:11–13, KJV)

Because we were heading south, we had a lady with us from the church that was going out to visit relatives, and she did not want to fly, and so she hitched a ride with us. We were going to drop her off in Grand Prairie, Alberta, just about a day's drive.

We drove out to the end of the Pine Point entrance road and took one final look behind and said farewell to Pine Point. Thus began the nightmare, at least which is what the devil would have had us believe. We drove fifteen miles, and all of a sudden, the trailer started to sway back and forth from side to side. I stopped and got out to see if perhaps it was just a flat tire. Sure enough, it was a flat tire, but that was not all. The trailer was sitting on the ground, and when I looked under it, I saw the problem. The axle had broken! Fifteen miles out of town and a broken axle. What do we do now? I already knew that back in Pine Point, there were no trailers for sale, let alone a new axle. It was a nice day, and we had snacks and blankets, so I told everyone what the plan was. I said, "God called us to ministry and Bible college, and there is no way we are turning back." Besides, we had nothing to go back to. I would take the tires off the trailer and dismantle the axle and drive to Hay River forty-one miles ahead. There I would get it welded and bring it back and reinstall it, and we would be off again.

Everyone got out and headed off the road to the field beside the road, and that was where they waited while I did what I had to do. I had brought all my tools, and I was fairly good at mechanics, so it did not take long to get the axle off. I took the axle straight to the weld shop in Hay River, and the mechanic reinforced the axle and welded it together. There was no weld shop in the town of Pine Point, only out at the mine site, and they were not allowed to do private work. With the work done, I headed back to the family and the trailer and reinstalled the axle and tires. In total, the whole procedure took three hours, and we were mobile again.

We were driving along fine until we got to Hay River, fifty-five miles from Pine Point. As we were about to make our left-hand turn onto the highway leading south, the trailer hit the ground again. When I got out to see what was wrong, my heart sank a little. The weld had broken, and once again, the axle needed to be repaired. It was barely drivable but enough that we could drive to the same weld shop. The owner had a little laugh, and then he said, "You have way too much weight on that thing, and if you are going to try and drive it like that, you will need to drive fifty miles per hour." Well, that wasn't happening because we had four thousand miles to go. I asked him what he would suggest. He said the simple solution would be to put a bigger axle on it. Then he said, "I have a couple of those hardtop trailers in the back, but the bodies are damaged. We can get a bigger axle off one of them and put it on for you, but you will need to pay me for the whole trailer because once the axle is gone, it is of no use to me, and I was going to fix them and sell them." I agreed and bought the whole trailer just for the bigger axle. Another hour and a half, and we were on the road again.

We had left Pine Point at 11:00 a.m., six and a half hours earlier, and had only traveled fifty-five miles. We were still heading south, and that was all there was too it. Now we were able to at least do the speed limit and keep moving forward. It was about a hundred and sixty miles from Pine Point to the NWT border. Just inside the Alberta line, there was a little native restaurant and gas station, a pit stop. We decided we would make a pit stop there just so we could say we accomplished something by getting out of the North West Territories the same day we left. Well, there was the border in sight, and it was just getting dusk, and all of a sudden, there was a pile of sparks behind me. The next thing we saw was a small tire literally flying forward past the car. I stopped right away, and when I got out, I saw right away what was wrong. The wheel on the axle had separated from the axle and flew past the car and into the ditch. I was dumbfounded.

We could see the native store just ahead, so I drove the car to the side of the road as far as I could, dragging the trailer. Once there, I disconnected the trailer because it was now too dark, and you could not see much. We left the trailer right there and drove to the native stop. We spoke to the owner, and he said he had someone who could fix it for us, but he would not be back until morning. At that point, we had another decision to make—our passenger! We had found out that there was a bus coming through at six o'clock in the morning. So we bought her a ticket, and we ate, and then we all curled up in the car as best we could and waited out the night in the car. It was horrendous. Mosquitoes and heat, morning could not come soon enough. Six o'clock came, and after profusely apologizing to our rider, we put her on the bus, and away she went. (I guess it would have been less stressful for her if she had waited in Pine Point the extra day for the bus).

Now we wait. The mechanic never showed up until two in the afternoon, so we sat around all day doing nothing. We would walk, snooze, eat, walk, snooze, and eat. When he finally showed up, we followed his tow truck out to our trailer on the highway so he could pick it up. Also, I needed to walk down into the ditch and look for the tire that had come off and rolled into the ditch the night before. As we got to the trailer and turned the car around and got in behind the trailer, I kid you not, the car overheated because the water pump blew. So now the mechanic had to pick up our trailer on the back of his truck and then latch on to our car and tow us back to the native stop. He unhooked my car and the trailer in a spot out of the way, and then we went inside and ordered a water pump and a plate to fit the wheel back on the trailer. They told us they would put it on the bus, and it would arrive the next morning. Well, he had to work on our trailer outside because there was no garage. That made it a little more comfortable for us that night because we could set the trailer up and sleep in it. Also, the kids' bikes had been attached to the top of the trailer for transporting them so the kids could ride them around.

The day went by very slowly, and finally we went to sleep. The next morning, we waited for the bus, and when it came, the parts were not on the bus. Right away, we called the parts store, and they said they had trouble locating the water pump and wanted to send both parts together because it was cheaper, so they would send them in the morning now that they had both of them. Well, frustration was setting in, and we tried to keep our distance from each other most of the day, and I think you can understand why.

I Told You So

Later that afternoon, I was lying on the front seat of my car, and the next thing I saw was the face of Pastor Ritchie Hayward. He poked his head into the car and smiled and said, "I told you so! You are not called to go into ministry." I simply said, "This is a minor test. I'll call you when I get to Bible college." We laughed, and all of us went inside and had supper together, and we told him our bizarre story of how we got here. Pastor Hayward was on his way to Edmonton for a conference and just stopped in for gas and spotted us. He said he could not resist the temptation to say what he did, but he said he also realized God does things His way. Then he left. The parts came the next morning at 6:00 a.m., and by noon the mechanic had fixed the trailer, and I had done the water pump myself.

We headed out and down the road. We felt a sense of relief as we drove. We went another 240 miles without incident and started to feel good about how things were going until the tire on the car went flat. Well, that was normal to us because living in the north on dirt roads, you expect it. I had a spare tethered to the top of the tent trailer under the bikes, but when I went to take it down, it was flat. Living in the north, you learn to expect that too. But what we did not expect was when I took everything out of the trunk and took the second spare tire out, it was flat too! There were so many emotions going through my heart and mind at that moment that I was not sure if I should yell or cry. I had no choice. It was sixty miles farther south to Peace River, and that was where I needed to go to get the tires fixed. I took both tires and rolled them down the road about fifty yards so I would be seen when a vehicle came along. Three vehicles passed me before a man in a pickup stopped and picked me and the tires up. We drove to Peace River and got them fixed, and the garage owner was a nice person and took me and the tires back out to the road so I could hitch back. It took half an hour before someone finally stopped and gave me a ride back. It was three and a half hours turnaround time, and the car was ready to go. *"Knowing this, that the trying of your faith worketh patience"* (James 1:3, KJV).

Taking Authority

Just before we started the car and got back on the road, I said to my family, "We need to do something that we should have done a long time ago. Everybody out of the car and let's surround the car. Put your hands on the car, and I am going to pray." Then I prayed, "Lord, You called us to ministry. We have no doubt. You have provided everything, and we are trusting You. The devil has tried his best to stop us, and now, Lord, we are asking You to put a stop to his antics. Satan, we take authority over you in the name of Jesus, and we plead the blood of Jesus over us and this car and trailer. Take your hands off us and the car and the trailer because this is God's property you are messing with. We thank You, Lord, for Your protection. In Jesus's name." From that moment on, there was never another problem. We completed the rest of the trip without so much as a hiccup. Thank You, Jesus. God is faithful. *"For He shall give His angels charge over you, To keep you in all your ways. In their hands they shall bear you up, Lest you dash your foot against a stone"* (Psalm 91:11–12, NKJV).

An Uncertain Visit

Before we headed east to Peterborough, Ontario, where the Bible college is located, we felt we would go west and see my sister Mary and also make an effort to talk to my parents one more time because we had no idea when and if we would ever get out this way again, and we did not know if we would ever have the opportunity to speak to them again. The memory of my last visit was still fresh in my mind of picking up Mary to take back to Pine Point and being rejected by Mom and Dad. However, I thought maybe it would be different this time because God had called me into ministry. I thought maybe they would be proud of me for taking that direction. I could never have been so wrong.

We made the trip in two days, and we arrived at my parents' place late in the afternoon. My father met me at the door, and as per usual, he had been drinking. He said, "Why are you here?" I said, "Because you are my parents, and I would still like a relationship with you both." He said, "You can park your car and trailer in the back and look after yourself for food and sleeping. Maybe later I will talk to you because, as a matter of fact, I have something to discuss with you." I was taken aback by his comments but thought at least he was willing to speak to me this time. I parked the car and set up the trailer and then took the family downtown to eat. When we got back, he was sitting outside on the porch, so I went up to him and said, "Dad, before you say anything, there is something I want to tell you." He did not answer; he just stared at me. I guess he was waiting for me to say what was on my mind, so I did. I said, "Dad, I accepted Christ as my Savior, and God has called me to be a minister. I am on my way to Bible college in Ontario."

At that moment, he stood up, and I could see that familiar anger in his eyes. He said, "After all the trouble I went through to get you an invite to join the Masons, you pull this on me. I was going to call you and tell you I can get you in the Masons and get you a real good job as well instead of messing around in the dirty old mines. Why the h—— would you want to be part of a bunch of people who eat babies?" (I think he was referring to child sacrifices in the Bible back in the Old Testament, I'm not sure). Then he went on to say, "Look, if you give up that nonsense and join the Masons, you will be set for life." I said, "I can't do that, Dad. I gave my life to Christ, and I intend to follow Him as long as I live." At that point, he made a comment that I did not understand until much later. He said, "If you are not going to renounce that garbage, then you will need to get out of my life for good before I do what I am required to do." (I studied the Masons for seven years straight after that and found out things that shocked me, things like what he said. He could make someone disappear if they challenged or slandered or converted to Christianity from the Masons.) I did not know it at the time, but Dad was the grandmaster of British Columbia, and I guess my getting saved and turning down the offer to join the Masons was egg on his face. He wanted to save face, but I was not giving up Christ. He stopped talking and went in the house. I spent some time with my sister Mary, and then Daphne and the kids and I got in our tent trailer, and we tried to sleep. An hour later, I said to Daphne, "This is no good. Let's get out of here," and so we did. We packed up and were gone in twenty minutes. I would not see my father again for twenty-seven years. My mother died in 1999, and I found out by accident in 2000 that she had passed, so I never saw her again.

We drove until near midnight and parked. We quickly set up the trailer again and went to sleep. The next morning, we prayed and put everything behind us and headed for Ontario and Bible college.

> Not that I have already attained, or am already per-fected; but I press on, that I may lay hold of that for which Christ Jesus has also laid hold of me. Brethren, I do not count myself to have apprehended; but one thing I do, forgetting those things which are behind and reaching forward to those things which are ahead, I press toward the goal for the prize of the upward call of God in Christ Jesus. (Philippians 3:12–14, KJV)

Just as a footnote to this, you may want to keep the above story in mind when you read on. Twenty-seven years changes a lot of things, and the change that comes about can only happen because God designs it. I know you will be blessed by it.

CHAPTER 7

College Delayed

A New Pastor

The rest of the trip was uneventful, and a few days later, we arrived in Pickering, Ontario, at Daphne's aunt's house. She was gracious and allowed us to set up our camper in her driveway. It was June, so the outside temperature was warm enough. We didn't keep the trailer long. We had been through enough with it so getting rid of it was no problem in our minds. We sold it a week later and moved into Aunt Charlotte's basement apartment where we were to stay until the end of August. We settled in and did nothing for the next few days except sit around and relax and recuperate from the trip.

Sunday was coming, and we searched out the Pentecostal church in Pickering and made our way over to it on Sunday morning. We met the pastor and his wife, Reverend Willard and Carolyn Whitman. They were very nice to us and welcomed us into the church. We got to know them and spent some time with them. We have been through many interesting times together since then, and we have been extremely close friends ever since.

Stalled

Well, the reason we were in Ontario was to go to Bible college, so I purchased a Thompson Chain-Reference Bible, which I have and use to this day. I bought it in preparation to go to Bible college. Then the first part of July, I needed to go to Peterborough and register to start the first semester in college. So I drove to Peterborough and found the college. Once I was there, I parked and walked up to the front door. There was no one around, and all seemed quiet—that is, until I reached the front door. Before I went in, I noticed a newspaper box by the front door and a newspaper facing out with the headline showing. That headline changed everything. What I saw sent shivers down my back, and uncertainty filled my heart. The town of Peterborough's population was in the low sixty thousands and not much industry in the town except for the normal things like grocery stores, gas stations, and the like. It was also home to Outboard Marine, the largest employer in the town. It employed most of the working force, about ten thousand. The headline read, "Outboard Marine Lays Off Five Thousand."

I froze with my hand on the doorknob to the college. In a split second, so many scenarios flew through my mind. The main thought I had was, how am I going to support my family? You see, I had planned on working and going to college as well. But with five thousand laid off, my mind could not wrap itself around how I would get a job with so many others looking as well. A lot of other things went through my mind, but in the end, just seconds later, I purchased a newspaper to take home and show my wife. Then I left the college and drove back home deflated. At that moment, I had let the devil play me. My new Bible was right beside me and taunting me. It will come in handy down the road though!

After explaining to Daphne my thoughts, we decided we would look for work and wait until things picked up, and I could go to college. We both found work in Whitby, which was ten and a half miles farther east of Pickering. Once we found the work, we needed to move over there so we would be closer, and we found an apartment and became the building superintendents which paid the rent. School for the kids was just up the road, so it worked out well. God was still leading even though I was stalled and waffling on going to college.

Now the hard part. We needed to go to Pastor Whitman and tell him we were moving and that there was a Pentecostal church only half a mile from where we were living. We had only known Willard and Carolyn for a short time, but we had fallen in love with them. As a matter of fact, as I have already said, we have remained the best of friends ever since. We have been through many hard times together with sickness on both sides, theirs and ours, but we have stuck together and supported each other. So it really was no surprise when we told them we were moving that their grace showed. They were not upset but rather very supportive and said to us that it was the right thing to do: support the local church. He agreed that it did not make sense to travel that distance when the church was practically in our yard.

We moved. The kids started school in Whitby. We began attending Whitby Pentecostal Church, and we had another wonderful pastor: Reverend David and Sally McLean. He was also a powerful teacher/preacher, and he went out of his way to visit us and make us feel welcome. The Whitby church was much like the church we had left in Pine Point. We made friends with families that had children our children's age, and we began visiting just like we did in the north. Many of those friends as well have now gone on to be with the Lord, but many others we still keep in touch with and see often.

Without going into a lot of detail concerning the next five years, suffice it to say they were hard on me and us. I knew I was supposed to be in ministry, and I was not making the effort because now I was back where I had started before going to Pine Point, Northwest Territories. Going from one job to another, and I was just making excuses not to go because I was convincing myself I could not support my family if I went.

That is until one Sunday night at church. I was under so much conviction. God had been dealing with my heart for the last few weeks, and I was restless in my spirit. I was at church, and I spoke to Joe Hoskins, a friend and a board member. The Pentecostal church we were attending had a few problems after Reverend David McClean left, and it caused us to move from the Pentecostal church over to a nondenominational church. It was a big eighteenth-century building. They had put an octopus-type furnace in the cellar, and it had a big space where you could go and sit down if you wanted to be alone. I told Joe what was going on in my life, and he said, "Let's go down to the furnace room and talk. It's quiet and private." Once we went down and sat on the benches, I opened up my heart to him. I told him about the call, the layoffs at Outboard Marine, the jumping from job to job, and finally getting a job that was paying extremely well. I told him I was torn between going to Bible college because I had rebelled for so long, and keeping the job I now had because I was making five grand a month. He said, "Prayer is no good unless you have made up your mind that you truly want God's plan and not yours." He was right. I said, "What if I put out a sort of fleece." He asked me what I would put before God, and I said, "Well, I have an idea. The job I have is paying very well, and the company is pleased with me. So what if I said if God has me fired from my job in the next week, I will take that as a definite sign." Joe laughed at that and said, "Nothing is too hard for God, but with that kind of fleece, it almost sounds like you don't want to give in and go to college." I said, "I just thought if I make it a real hard fleece, and maybe a ridiculous one, that if it did happen, it would definitely be God." So Joe prayed for me, and we left it with God. I felt in my spirit that it was the end of my wanting to go to Bible college because of how well I was doing at work.

Well, God has a sense of humor—I kid you not! The next morning, I went to work. I was the manager of the shop, and I was the guy who opened the place up. My office was locked by me, and I had the only key, so I thought. I went to work, and when I got there, the door was unlocked, and the lights were on. If that was not creepy enough, my office door was open. My first thought was a break-in. That is, until I walked into my office, and there sitting behind my desk in my chair was the superintendent of the district I was working in. His name was Phil. No last name to protect him. I looked at him and said, "What are you doing here? How did you get in?"

Before I go on, let me take you back to Friday before the weekend. The superintendent (Phil) had come to the office as he normally did on a Friday to collect all the contracts for the sales we had made. This particular month, we had done very well, and I was going to get a good bonus along with my salary. About five thousand dollars salary and bonus before taxes. That did not seem to be enough for Phil. He said, "Bob, we can do better and get an even bigger bonus for each of us and set an all-time record for sales." Then he presented me his plan. He said, "Here's what I want you to do. I want you to sign off on these four contracts for sales to —— (then he named a hospital in a nearby town). If we put them through before Monday at 9:00 a.m., we will get the bonuses and set the record." What he was asking me to do was to lie and put the sales through as being sold to a hospital that did not even exist, in a town not even big enough to support a hospital anyway. He said, "The company does not know that, and we can cancel the contracts a week later, but by then, all the paperwork on bonuses and records will be done." I said to him, "Phil, I can't do that. It is lying. We have done enough for this month, and next month has a lot more prospects to do even better." He was not happy, and he said, "You need to think this over very carefully and let me know on Monday early." It never entered my mind during that conversation that he would think about firing me, so I said, "I will think it through and let you know."

Now it was nine o'clock Monday morning, and I was standing at the front of my desk, and he was sitting behind my desk. The contracts were still sitting on my desk and were unsigned, and I was not signing them. I never said a word about them. So I asked, "What are you doing here? How did you get in?" The next words out of Phil's mouth literally made me burst out laughing. He said, "Bob, you are fired!" I mean it—I laughed out loud, and that made him angry. He said, "What are you laughing for?" I said, "Well, first of all, why are you firing me?" He said, "Because of that!" he said as he pointed to a calendar on the wall. The calendar was a standard-sized calendar, and it was hanging on a nail. But also on the nail I had hung a four-inch-by-three-inch wooden wall plaque with the picture of Jesus on it. It was barely visible against the background of the picture on the calendar. I said, "What's wrong with that?" He said, "The employees in this shop are offended by it." I giggled some more because I knew full well it was a cover-up excuse for not signing the contracts. He could not justify firing me for not signing the contract, so he needed an out for his own "protection." But I never expected to get fired for it.

The plaque

At this point, all I wanted to do was pick up my stuff and get out of there because I immediately recognized an answer to prayer, and it was not going to change. Phil was still not impressed because he said, "I want to know what you are laughing at." I said, "Phil, you did not fire me. You just fulfilled the will of God." His face turned a bright red, so much so that I thought he was going to explode. I did not even get into any type of discussion with him. And as I was leaving, I said, "Well, Phil, the only thing I need from this office is my picture and my final check." That was when he got nasty. He said, "No way, I need to confiscate your commissions and bonus to pay the office bills. Your leaving is putting us under a lot of pressure and in a bind"—like it was my doing! He was not going to give me my check, so I left.

God Steps In

God was not done with this. I went home and told Daphne what had happened. She was excited that God had answered prayer, but she was hopping mad at Phil because he would not pay us. She said, "He is taking food right off our table." We prayed and turned it over to God, and we left it with Him. We did not see anyone from the church until Wednesday when we went to Bible study. We gathered in a room for the study, and like I said, we had not breathed a word to anyone. Before the study started, the pastor opened in prayer. He no sooner finished, and there was a message in tongues, and an interpretation followed. This was unusual for our Bible study, and it was the first time it had happened since we had been attending. The interpretation made both Daphne and me laugh and feel such a sense of God's overwhelming care that it is hard to explain. The interpretation was simple: "I have seen your trouble. I am your provider. I will fight this battle for you." How much plainer could it be? We explained to the group in Bible study what had happened from the time Joe had prayed with me to the firing and the interpretation.

We went home rejoicing. God did provide for us, and before I continue with getting to Bible college, let me just tell you that less than six weeks later, Phil was arrested, went to jail for fraud, and lost his job. God said, *"I will take revenge; I will pay them back. In due time their feet will slip. Their day of disaster will arrive, and their destiny will overtake them"* (Deuteronomy 32:35, NLT).

The Application

God had set things in motion. I knew He was opening the door for me to go to Bible college because I was finally obeying. The first thing I needed to do was go and put my application in at the college and get approved and go. Simple. Not really!

I went to the Bible college and filled out the necessary paperwork and application. By the way, this time, I ignored the newspaper box. I delivered the application to the office and had a short interview to go over the paperwork. They told me the admissions committee would meet and discuss the application and let me know in a few days. They said their decision would dictate if I would be called for a full-scale interview. I went back to Whitby to wait it out. Three days later, I received a telephone call from the Bible college vice president. He asked me if I could come in for an interview the next morning, and I said yes. I was totally excited that we had gotten this far. I was going in for the full interview. This was a promising sign!

The next morning, I was in Peterborough bright and early. I was called into the interview room, and then the grilling began. I was asked why I thought I should go to Bible college. How did I receive my call? What made me so sure I was called to ministry? Had I prayed about it? Could I do something else besides going to Bible college to become a minister? And a few other questions that one would normally expect to defend their position. Then the interview changed and became what I thought to be antagonistic. Why was I not attending a Pentecostal church? Did I believe in the Pentecostal message? What prompted me to go to an independent church? Did I believe in the gifts of the Spirit, more specifically speaking in tongues as the initial evidence of the baptism?

The interview left me bewildered and uncertain as to whether I was going to be accepted or not. They had intimated that they were prone to accepting Pentecostal people who attended Pentecostal churches, not independent churches. That sounded very elitist to me, but I assured them I was a Pentecostal through and through and that I only attended the independent work in Whitby because there were no other Pentecostal churches in Whitby. I also told them they were well aware of the problems the Whitby church was having and of the many people from the Whitby church who were also attending the same independent work we were until the situation at the Whitby Pentecostal church was fixed. I told them they could check my records at the Pentecostal church, and they would see my record of giving and support for missions and missionaries. I told them they should ask the minister to whose house a visiting missionary and his family would go for lodging when they came to speak at the church, "always ours." Plus, there were many other things I suggested they could check out to see how through and through Pentecostal I/we are.

The interview ended, and they told me to go and have lunch and come back at 1:00 p.m., and they would have an answer. I did, and when I came back, I did not get in to see them until 2:00 p.m.

because they had not finished deliberating. Then they called me in, and to my surprise, they were very blunt. "Robert," the vice president spoke, "we are sorry, but because of your present affiliation, we are unable to grant you acceptance to the college. We would suggest you find a Pentecostal church and get plugged in and then apply in a year." I was blown away. I went home almost in tears but more angry in spirit—yes, angry that they would be that biased and, more so, challenge my loyalty to the Pentecostal movement. When I got home, I talked it over with Daphne, and I said to her, "God called me to that college, and He opened too many doors for man to shut them." It was 4:00 p.m., and I felt so strong in my spirit that they were wrong that I called the college and asked to speak to the vice president. I was fortunate. He was still there, and surprisingly he took my call.

The Telephone Call

This was my conversation with him, and I believe it was a God-led conversation. I said, "Brother ———, I would like you to listen to what I have to say, and please let me finish before you say anything." He said, "Yes, go ahead." I continued, "Brother ———, God called me to ministry. He called me when I was in a Pentecostal church that I supported with my tithes and supported missionaries and still do. I served on the board and taught Sunday school. I went through many trials to get here. I moved from the Whitby church to an independent church to protect my children from the nonsense that was going on in the Whitby church. We told the pastor we would be back when the mess was sorted out. He said he understood, and hopefully it would clear up quickly so we could all return to fellowship. We went with his blessing. There was no other Pentecostal church close for us to attend. Recently, we received a confirmation to go to Bible college via tongues and interpretation. My wife and I are Spirit-filled. We speak in tongues as the Spirit gives us utterance. God called me to Eastern Pentecostal Bible college, and I know I am supposed to be there. I ask you to reconsider. I told him that I was done, and he said thank you for the call, and they would get back to me.

One hour later at 5:20 p.m., the telephone rang, and it was the vice president of the college again. He said, "Brother Coutts, after reconsidering your request, we have agreed to admit you to the college." No explanation or apology, just right to the point, which was fine by me. I said thank-you and hung up. I told Daphne and bawled my eyes out. Right away I called Joe Hoskins, the board member and friend who had prayed for me. He was just as excited for me as I was for myself. That night, we took the kids and went out to celebrate. God does not make mistakes.

Sometimes you need to know in your spirit that something is the right thing to do. This was the right thing for us. God had brought us too far to drop us. Maybe you are in that same boat. The whole idea of what I have written is to show you that God knows exactly what He is doing. He has every step planned. "The steps of a good man are ordered by the LORD: and he delighteth in his way" (Psalm 37:23). Leaning on Christ becomes a way of life, and He said if you do that, He would never leave you nor forsake you. The week fairly flew by, and when Sunday came, we were excited to go to church and share with everyone what God had done.

An Hilarious Provision

We went to church on Sunday and shared the story with everyone, and they all shared our excitement. We had a wonderful day in the Lord. That evening, Daphne and I were lying in bed unable to sleep because of the great day we had in church and the excitement we felt about what God was doing. As we lay there I turned to Daphne and I said, "You know, there is one consideration we have not laid hold of yet." She said, "What is that?" I said, "We don't have a car!" We both laughed and said, "Well, God has never failed us, and He has not brought us this far to say it's over. And we do have a little while before the first semester starts." So we talked a little more, and then Daphne said, "I have an idea." I laughed and said, "That could be dangerous." She said, "No! listen. We have been memorizing a scripture about waiting on the Lord. You know the one: 'But they that wait upon the LORD shall renew their strength; they shall mount up with wings as eagles; they shall run, and not be weary; and they shall walk, and not faint' (Isaiah 40:31). And do you remember Gideon in the Bible? He put out a fleece before God. Why don't we do the same? We ask God to provide a car, and we will know it is his provision by the sign of an eagle. You know, wait on the Lord and mount up as wings of eagles." We both laughed again, but the first thought that went through my mind was a Trans Am because it had a great big eagle on the hood. I could see me driving a Trans Am! That brought a giggle out of both of us too. We agreed on the eagle and prayed and asked God if He would help us with a vehicle and confirm it with the sign of an eagle. It was 12:30 a.m., so we thought we should go to sleep even though we were still excited.

What I am about to tell you is a miracle, and it is funny at the same time. We were lying in bed trying to go to sleep, and suddenly we could hear what sounded like a jingling out in our living room on the front window. It startled us, and we just lay there for a moment. It repeated, so we got out of bed and went to the living room, and we could see something at our front window. We got closer for a look, and there, through the window, we saw Joe Hoskins. He had a big smile on his face, and he was rattling some keys on our window and beckoned for us to come out on the porch.

We were in our PJs, so out we went. Joe handed us the keys, and when we asked what they were for, he turned and pointed at a car at the end of the driveway, not a new one but a good-looking used one. His wife was sitting in their van waiting for him. We asked what this was all about, and he simply said, "For the last week, God has been dealing with me about giving you this car. I fought it until tonight, and after church was over, I knew you were going to need one to go to Bible college, and God said I was to give it to you. So here it is, it's yours." He handed us the ownership and a bill of sale which said "paid in full." Then he said, "We have to go. I have work in the morning. God bless you and enjoy the car." Then he left, and we had not even had a chance to look at the car or even say thank you. Joe left, and Daphne stayed on the porch while I walked to the end of the driveway to inspect the car. It had not even been two hours since we prayed. However, we were a bit skeptical because there was no sign of an eagle that would confirm our acquisition—that is, until I approached the car.

As I walked around the front of the car, I stopped dead in my tracks, and shivers went up and down my spine. There, right in the middle of the car on its front end, was a hood ornament in the shape of an eagle. I kept walking toward the driver's door, and again I stopped dead in my tracks. There on the back pillar was a decorative swirl with a circle in the center and the head of an eagle in it. That meant there was another one on the other side, so I went to look. Daphne must have thought I was inspecting the car by walking around it. As I rounded the back of the car, you could have knocked me over with a feather. The taillight of the car stretched from one side to the other, and right in the middle of the taillight was another emblem. It was another eagle.

Replica of the Miracle Ford Thunderbird given to us

I literally ran around to the driver's door and waved at Daphne to come out to the car. She did, and I showed her each emblem, and by now we were laughing and crying at the same time. I said, "This is called a Ford Thunderbird, and a thunderbird is an eagle! Let's take it for a quick ride around the block." She agreed, and we locked our front door because the kids were sleeping, and we got in the car. We took off driving around the block, and being a residential area, it was very dark, so I put the high beam on. I let out a shout because right there in the middle of the dash was a blue high-beam indicator light, and it was the head of an eagle! That was five eagles in total. To us, that was a confirmation for each member of our family. All five of us!

To top it off, the car was loaded to the teeth: sunroof, power everything, stereo cassette player, power seats, windows, air-conditioning, and more stuff than I can write down here. It was top of the line! God gives the best! We finished our ride and parked and went in the house and prayed and thanked God for supplying our need and especially so fast. We asked Him to bless Joe Hoskins right out of his socks for being obedient to the voice of God. We never did sleep much that night. Insurance was cheap, so we got it the next day, and we were set for Bible college. We made a call to Joe Hoskins and, the best way we knew how, thanked him for listening to the leading of the Lord.

But my God shall supply all your need according to his riches in glory by Christ Jesus. (Philippians 4:19, KJV)

CHAPTER 8

Studying Hard

Peterborough, Ontario

Well, the next couple of months could not go fast enough. While we were waiting for the first day of college, we needed to get all our affairs in order, clean up bills, get transfers for the kids from their school, and Daphne needed to give notice at work. We needed to travel to Peterborough, Ontario, where the college was located and start searching for a place to live. It was a busy time. We managed to get everything done, and then the last thing on the list was finding a place to live in Peterborough. So we left that to the last so we could concentrate on it. There really was no need because God had already gone before us, and when we got to Peterborough, we bought the local newspaper; and when we looked through it, we found a three-bedroom house right off the bat. It was in a good location not far from the college, and grocery stores were close by as well. We contacted the owner, looked at the house, and rented it. Our money was going fast, and at this point, we needed to take a breath and look at our situation.

The Realization

Now, do you remember when I told you that I came to the college in 1977 and that I was standing at the door holding the doorknob and reading the newspaper headlines on the paper in the newspaper box at the college entrance? "Outboard Marine Lays Off Five Thousand"? Here it was a few years later, and we had rented a house, moved our stuff, changed all our bill addresses, changed our driver's license addresses, transferred the kids' school papers, done everything necessary for the move, and we had no income or source of income. We did have enough money to last us about three months if we budgeted right. The rest, we knew, was up to God. It was even less than when I came the first time. The difference this time was that God had taken charge of my mind. I had allowed the devil to convince me the last time that I could not make it without doing something myself, like get a job. This time was different. God had showed us that He is able to supply what we need, from a car to a house to anything necessary to fulfill His plan for us. This time, we were here totally by faith! The funny thing about it was, we did not have a worry in the world because God had worked out so many of the hard details ahead of us.

The house was ours, and we moved in and settled in. The kids were registered in the local school, and we settled back to watch God plan our days. That was exactly what He did. The local Pentecostal church was just about a mile and a half from the house, and it was the first place we went. There we met a new pastor: Reverend Paul Starratt. He was a Nova Scotian like Daphne, and they hit it off right away. To jump ahead a bit so that I don't confuse the story, we did get involved heavily in the church. We went to everything they had: both Sunday services, Bible studies, prayer meetings, special events, We taught Sunday school and joined the men's and ladies' groups. We loved it a lot!

College at Last

College started, and it was then that reality set in. There was no possible way I would be able to hold down a job and attend college and do all the required courses and studies at the same time. That could have been the reason back in 1977 when I turned away not knowing these things. But God knew, and perhaps He allowed me to turn away until I turned to Him. Thank You, Lord, for Your patience with me. I can be pretty thick-headed and even opinionated, but, Lord, You knew. Thank You, Lord.

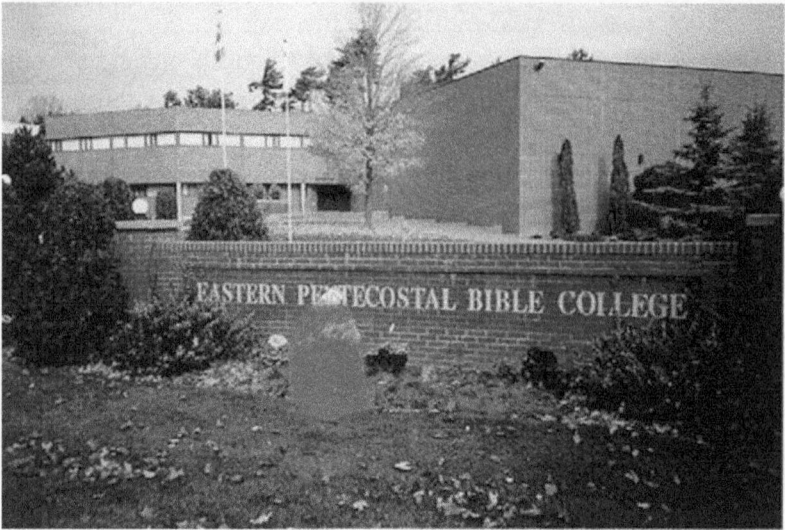

Eastern Pentecostal Bible College

The college load was pretty heavy. It required thirty-three hours of credits per semester, which translates to ten courses per semester. Each course required papers to be written, plus periodic tests to be studied for. There was no time for a full-time job. We had budgeted carefully and had included the first semester's fees and books, which left us without a whole lot of money. Our only income at that time was a family allowance that the government provided. It amounted to $33 per child, so we received $99. But in keeping with the way the Lord was working things out, it was almost immediate that we received a call from the college administrator. Her name was Ulva, and she wanted to speak with Daphne. She said, "Daphne, I have an elderly father with a very sick wife. They need help looking after their place because my father cannot do it. Can you? They will pay you for it." Daphne said yes because our children would be in school all day, and Ulva's parents wanted someone during the day. That started a chain reaction. Ulva knew someone else that needed someone to clean, and that person knew someone else, and so on. Daphne ended up with a list of people's places to clean and all during the time the kids were in school. It was enough money to keep us afloat and at least pay the bills. God just kept providing for us. The first semester was going along smoothly, and I was studying hard, and Daphne was cleaning during the day. I was even afforded a few opportunities on the weekend to fix some of the students' cars, and they would pay me for it, which added to our income.

Revival

Before I go too much further, I need to bring you up to date on something that happened at the college right from the start of the first semester. The college had just appointed a new president: Reverend Robert Taitinger. The first week of college was basically orientation and getting things in place so we could get down to the business of learning. The second week, we started off with chapel, and the speaker that morning was Reverend Robert Taitinger. We sang a few songs, and then Reverend Taitinger spoke. What happened next changed everyone's life. When he finished speaking, the Holy Spirit began to move. There was a message in tongues and an interpretation. The power of it drove half the student body to the altar. As students were going to the altar, they were slain in the spirit and literally falling on top of one another. Some began laughing hysterically in the spirit. Some sang in tongues; some were weeping uncontrollably. The chapel had started at 10:00 a.m., and by 1:00 p.m. the chapel was still full, and those things I described above continued.

Well, you would think it would have tapered off, and we would get back to school concerns. But no, the atmosphere in the chapel did not change. As a matter of fact, it intensified. No one led any songs, no one took the microphone, no one led anything. The Holy Spirit orchestrated everything, and a revival broke out. It continued on into the night. I myself felt I should go home and at least check in with my wife and kids. When I got home, I told her what was going on, but she had already heard. She asked me if I wanted something to eat, and all I could think of to say was, "Honey, I need to go back to the college." I did go back, and for the next six days for twenty-four hours a day, the same thing continued in the chapel. No one tried to stop it, and the college officials were even a part of it as well.

Some of the married students wanted their children to experience the revival, so they would bring them to the chapel. The amazing thing that happened was that these children as young as four and five and up were also slain in the spirit. You knew it was real because they would stay down under the power of the Holy Spirit for half an hour or more without moving. We started getting calls from across Canada of relatives of the students getting saved and healed. One night, some of the students went outside the chapel in order to eat. They ordered a pizza, and when the pizza delivery person showed up, he wanted to know what was going on. He said he could feel something powerful, and would it be okay to take a peek in the chapel? He was given the okay, and that was all it took. He went inside, and the Holy Spirit got hold of him, and he accepted Christ as his Savior without anyone touching or talking to him. He came back every night, and when it was over, he started going to the Pentecostal church in Peterborough.

Well, that revival lasted for six full days. Night and day, people were getting healed and saved.

> *And it shall come to pass in the last days, saith God,*
> *I will pour out of my Spirit upon all flesh: and your*
> *sons and your daughters shall prophesy, and your*
> *young men shall see visions, and your old men shall*
> *dream dreams.* (Acts 2:17, KJV)

It was a time of God instilling His love in us and preparing us for what was to come. Faith became a way of life because of it, and as I continue this story, you will see many times where God honored faith. It is awesome

Miracles in Abundance

The revival never really stopped. It migrated to the local churches, and things were happening on a continuing basis. Even at the college, some of our classes would start on time, and when we would open in prayer, it would develop into a whole session of prayer and seeking God. Sometimes we accomplished no schoolwork but received an anointing from the Lord.

All along, you can see how God has been leading, guiding, and preparing. That's what He does. If you are having trouble with direction in your life, I just know that God wants to sort it out for you. He leads in ways we cannot imagine, and usually it works out in spite of our own efforts. If you are struggling and not sure of the next step, I encourage you to trust God that He knows what is best. As I have progressed through this journey, you can see that God has had His hand on me and my family every step of the way. We did not always know it, and you won't always know it either. But when you put it all together, God has a superior plan, and He will never fail you.

What I would like to share with you now are some of the miracles that happened while in college. I have to tell you, though, it was hard to sort out the ones I wanted to share because there were so many. There were so many that Daphne and I bought a seventeen-by-fourteen-inch scrapbook to record them. Well, we filled a few pages, and then we decided—there were so many and it was so common and we couldn't even keep up with it, so we stopped. Today we wish we had continued because it would have been a book in itself. I will give you five of the top miracles, and I trust that in reading them, you will see that God was ever present and never put our family in jeopardy at any time. He was in total control and had everything planned down to the letter. In most cases, the miracles touched other lives, as well as our family. It opened my eyes to a bigger picture. The things that God does in our lives are examples for others as well, and they are used to speak to them and hopefully change their lives. I hope they encourage you and maybe even help change your life. He said everything will be all right, and these miracles are just some of the proof.

Tuition Paid

College was progressing nicely, and I was getting assignments done and tests completed. It was getting close to the end of the semester, and I had been praying about my next semester's tuition. Where was I going to get the money to continue with my studies? I knew that it had to come from the Lord, so I was continually in prayer concerning it. There was about a week left before I needed to take care of the payment; and when I came to the college that morning, I checked my mailbox. In it was a note from the president for me to come to his office before class started. So I made my way to his office, and he invited me in and said, "Please sit."

Then he said, "Robert, I have something here that was mailed to the college from British Columbia (that's the west coast of Canada). But that is all I can tell you because the people who sent this letter want to remain anonymous." Next he said, "What I can tell you is that inside is your tuition paid for the next semester." I was blown away and said to Reverend Taitinger, "I have been praying for weeks about this, and here God had it already planned." Reverend Taitinger said, "I can share this with you. They said in their letter that they had heard about you from a student in the college. And that student had shared how you had touched his life with your simple faith and how you lived it every day. He shared that with this couple, and in turn they have decided this is what they want to do for you." What could I say except, *Thank You, Lord!* I went to Bible college for a three-year ministerial diploma course, and I actually completed it in two years. But during those two years, I was called into the office many times to be told this amount was sent for my tuition or that amount, and in all, it was paid completely. I had paid the initial first semester's tuition; but after that, God supplied every cent by other people.

Then it happened. The last semester approached, and once again, I was praying about paying it. I was totally dependent on God because I did not have the extra cash to pay it myself. Well, this last time, it came down to the wire. The college had adopted a no-pay-on-faith policy. What I mean by that was, they were not going to let anyone write their final exams unless they had their tuition paid in full ahead of time. It seems they believed in faith, but they did not want us to practice it where their money was concerned. If that sounds harsh or cynical, I apologize; but considering I had been practicing faith and I was not presuming on God, this was a bit of a blow to me. I guess the administration just wanted to make sure they got their money up front. This caused me a bit of concern because God had provided everything, and I doubted He was going to stop now. The college had made an arrangement with the local credit union for students to borrow the money from them for tuition, and the college would cosign for the student.

The day came that tuition had to be paid, and they had set up tables in the chapel with loan officers available to complete the transactions. I was not comfortable in doing this, but I went into the chapel and picked up an application and sat at a desk. I wrote my name on the first line, and then I froze. I sat there for a few minutes and prayed and said, "Lord. You have never let me down, and I doubt You will now. I am not going to fill this out. I trust You to supply before this day ends." Then I was just about to get up and leave without filling out the forms, and there was a tap on my shoulder. I turned to see a fellow student Donald Brown. He said to me, "What are you doing, Bob?" I said, "Nothing. I am not doing this. I am going home." He said, "Oh, that's good because I don't want to have to tear up this certified check."

I looked at it, and I nearly wept on the spot. My name was on the "pay to the order" line, and the full amount of my last month's tuition was written on the next line. He said, "I had a couple of extra jobs this past couple of weeks, and it is more than I need, so I felt God telling me to do this for you." Don was an electrician by trade before coming to college. He had all the work he could handle while at college, and he shared with many students as God led him. I was one of the recipients. Again, I was amazed at God and at His timing. All I could say again was, *Thank You, Lord!*

> *But my God shall supply all your need according to his riches in glory by Christ Jesus.* (Philippians 4:19, KJV)

The Empty Oil Tank

The second most profound miracle that took place at college centered around our living accommodations. When our family first moved to Peterborough to go to Bible college, we had rented an old and very large four-bedroom brick house which was fairly near the college. We were not schooled in the art of checking things out before renting and did not realize this large house was heated by oil. The oil tank was in the basement, and the filler spout went out through the wall to the side of the house.

250-gallon oil tank

Now just let me back up for a moment and set the stage for what was about to happen. We went through a particularly lean month, and we did everything we could think of to save money on expenses. The end of the month came, and we had no money for electricity or oil. It was just starting to get real cold at night as well, so having three children, we thought we should act accordingly.

I went to the college dean and told him my circumstance, and he said there was a plan at the school to help married students. It was a loan directly from the school, and if I wanted it, all I had to do was ask. There was no interest, and it was a onetime-only loan which was required to be paid back by the end of the school year. The dean said he would make out the paperwork and write a check. We needed $1,100 to cover electricity; rent, which was $650 alone; and the rest of the house bills, which also included food. That amount would not provide for the oil, but we could run a space heater instead. Expensive, but we would manage. I told the dean I would go into the school chapel and wait for him. He agreed, and I went in and knelt down at the front pew to pray. The lights were dimmed, and no one was in the chapel, which made me feel better so I could tell the Lord my problem without being bothered. As I was praying, I heard someone walk up behind me and touch my shoulder. Immediately I turned around to see who it was, but there was no one there. It unnerved me a bit, but I went back to praying. The moment I began praying, the very same thing happened; only this time, the touch was stronger. Nobody was there, and I distinctly heard in my spirit, *Bob, everything's going to be all right.* I wept!

I stood up, and at that moment, I knew God was going to supply. Once again, He was assuring me that everything was going to be all right. As I approached the chapel door, it swung inward and hit me, pushing it outward. It was the dean. As soon as he saw my face, he said, "You don't want this, do you?" I said, "No!" He said, "Praise the Lord." Then he hugged me and tore up the check. Then he said, "Let me know how it works out, okay?" I smiled and agreed.

I left the college and headed home. When I arrived, I was walking up the sidewalk to the front door, and I heard steps behind me. When I turned around, there was a married student standing there in front of me with a smile. He said, "Bob, I am sorry. God told me to give this to you a week ago, and I got too busy." He then handed me an envelope and said, "I've got to go." As he left, I did not even get a chance to say anything to him or even open the envelope when another student came up the walk and handed me a book. He said, "Here is that book I promised you by Josh McDowell. It is called *Many Infallible Proofs*, and if you look on page 50, you will find fifty infallible proofs." He left as quickly as the other student. When they were gone, I opened the envelope to find $500 inside, and then I opened the book to page 50, and there was a $50 bill tucked inside. This was three o'clock in the afternoon. By the time 5:00 p.m. rolled around, I had a few more visitors, and the bottom line was, we had $1,210. That was $1,100 exactly for the bills and $110 for the tithes on the $1210. God is precise, on time, never fails, caring, and He has a sense of humor too. Isn't He great!

Well, we paid the bills and settled into our routine of meeting with friends and having singsongs and studies. It was October, and it had gotten particularly cold. We had a few people over, and the space heater was blasting. One of my closest friends in college, Darryl Bunn, was with us that night. As we were singing, a breaker blew that was controlling the heater. Darryl volunteered to go into the basement and reset it. When he got downstairs, he hollered back up to us and said, "Hey, Bob. Why don't you turn the furnace on?" I went to the top of the basement stairs and said, "Darryl, I would if we could afford oil." He said, "Well, I don't know how much more oil you would need than this full tank down here." At that point, I went down to take a look. I was totally shocked. There was a small puddle of oil on the top of the tank because the tank was over full. I said to Darryl, "How can that be? We did not order oil, and we certainly did not see a truck deliver it. Maybe the landlady ordered it, so I will call her in the morning." We fired up the furnace, and it warmed up nicely in no time.

The next morning, out of curiosity, I went outside to look at the oil inlet spout. What I saw caused me to get goose bumps. In order for the truck to load oil into the tank, they would need to back up onto the property, and in so doing, they would have left tracks in the snow. The snow around the inlet spout was pristine. Not a mark anywhere. On top of that, the inlet spout was covered in leaves which had fallen from the trees around it, and they were lodged in the curve of the spout right up to the filler cap. If oil had been delivered, the person delivering it would have needed to remove the leaves to get to the cap. On a whim, I tried the cap to see if oil was up to the top. I could not move the cap. It was literally rusted on. I went inside and told my wife all about the findings and said I better call the landlady. I called her, and she seemed quite upset. She said, "I didn't order oil, and if you have a full tank, you are paying for it, not me." And she hung up.

Well, now I was really intrigued. So I called every oil company in Peterborough and asked if they delivered oil. Not one of them delivered oil. We had been asking God to supply the means to obtain oil, and instead He filled the tank Himself. And because He filled the tank, it lasted longer than normal. The temperatures would hover between twenty below, ten below, and freezing all the time, so the furnace was constantly going. God filled the 250-gallon tank in the middle of October, and we never needed oil again until the middle of March. Five months. Fifty gallons a month, and normally it would have been 150 plus gallons a month for those temperatures and an old two-story, four-bedroom brick house.

> *The Lord is my shepherd; I shall not want. He makes me lie down in green pastures. He leads me beside still waters. He restores my soul. He leads me in paths of righteousness for his name's sake. Even though I walk through the valley of the shadow of death, I will fear no evil, for you are with me; your rod and your staff, they comfort me. You prepare a table before me in the presence of my enemies; you anoint my head with oil; my cup overflows.* (Psalm 23:1–6, KJV)

God poured out a blessing, all right. He poured it right into the oil tank, and there was hardly room for it because it was coming out the top.

Before I get to the next miracle, I want to make sure you are with me. The reason I am sharing these things is to show you God cares, and He truly does want everything to be all right, even with you. You may not experience dramatic miracles, but you will certainly experience the provision of God. No matter what you are going through, He is always there. It may not feel like it at times, but He is. I went into that chapel, and God showed Himself real and provided what I needed through other believers. He filled our oil tank. He provided. The best part is, He does it in His time, and He does it His way. Others are touched by what God does for us. They see the provision, and it provides hope and encouragement for them as well. So don't give up. I hope you are encouraged today. *"Trust in the Lord with all your heart, and lean not on your own understanding; In all your ways acknowledge Him, and He shall direct your paths"* (Proverbs 3:5–6, KJV).

Now we come to number three in the list of our favorite miracles.

The Rambler

Once we had settled into college life, we also started cutting a few corners. Going to college with three children and no job presented challenges we were not prepared for. One of those challenges was keeping a big car on the road with gas, insurance, and repairs. The Thunderbird was an awesome car, and it served us well for the first year and a half of college. Now it was becoming expensive to run, and we made a hard decision after praying much about it. We sold the car and used the money for rent, bills, and food. However, we still needed a car. We needed one that had a smaller, more efficient engine. Daphne and I talked and prayed much about it. I had an idea that was borne out of those prayers. It seemed foolish at first, but I told Daphne what I believed God was telling me to do. We needed a car that was excellent on gas, would not cost a lot to insure, and a car that was in good shape and not in need of mechanical repairs all the time.

I believe God told me in my spirit to sit down with the newspaper and circle ten cars that would seem to fit our criteria. It was funny at first and tempting to circle some of the fancier sports cars, but we knew better. Practicality was the order of the day. As I looked through the ads of cars, my eyes immediately fell on an advertisement for a 1976 Rambler. At first, I was tempted to bypass it, but the description caught my eye. It had new shocks, brake tires, and some new front-end parts. It was a six-cylinder (good on gas), new enough that it was not in need of more repairs, and not so old that the insurance would be high. I hesitated, but in the end, I circled it and put a number 10 beside it. I continued until I had circled 10 cars and numbered them in the order I liked them. Of course, the Rambler was last because I was still not impressed. I reasoned that God would give me something good—that is, something *I* considered good!

The next step was to pray over each one and also to ask God how we were going to pay for the car. The funny thing was, we were at peace and really did not worry about that part. The next thing we did was we called the numbers connected with each car. The strange thing that happened was that every car was either sold or no longer available, except *the* Rambler. When I called about the Rambler, a lady answered and said the car was still available, but I could not come and look at it until her husband came home. Would I please call back at 5:00 p.m.? I said to the lady, "I respect your request, and I will call at 5:00 p.m." I then said, "I am a Bible college student, married, and would feel more comfortable if your husband is home anyway." She said, "Oh, do you go to Eastern Pentecostal Bible College or another college in town?" (there were other Bible colleges as well). I told her I did, and also that I attended Northview Pentecostal Church. Then she said, "Really! Do you know my husband? He is a board member at Northview." I told her my name, she told me hers, and lo and behold, we had met at church.

I called back at 5:00 p.m. and set a time to meet with the husband. When I got to their house and we greeted, he took me to the garage and showed me the Rambler. I was amazed. It was immaculate. It had also just recently been painted. It looked amazing. I told him I really liked it, and I would like to have it. He said because I was a student, he would give it to me for $500, and I was ecstatic because it was worth much more than that. Then I asked him if he would hold it for two weeks because I had a few mechanics jobs lined up, and it would be enough to pay for it. He said, "No, but you can take it and pay for it when you have the money." Again I was totally amazed and could not believe what God had just done.

But that was not the end of it. The very next day, I was to go and get the car to bring it home, and I had gone to the Canadian Tire Store with Darryl my friend. While I was there, another student approached me and said, "Bob, I need your help. Can you put six spark plugs in my car and change the rear shocks?" It was about an hour's work, and I said sure. He said, "Good, here's the parts, and I will pay you now. Just leave the car at the college and leave the keys under the front seat." (He had to go somewhere and couldn't come to get the car or pay me before the evening, so he gave it to me in advance.) He left, and I looked at how much he gave me. It was $500 with a note: "God bless you." I went right to work and fixed his car and then went straight to the board member's house and paid him for the car and took it home. One final thing. We had moved from the big brick house to a newer government house. The address on the house was 559 Raymond Street. The license plate on the car was 559 RAY. I do not believe in coincidences. I believe in verifiable miracles, and this was one such verifiable miracle.

1976 Rambler

The Two Bags of Groceries

A while ago, I told you that I believe God also has a sense of humor. I don't believe it is a sense of humor in the practical joking sense but rather a sense of humor that, in the end, is beneficial to us because of what He accomplished. This next miracle is one of those cases. It was again another particularly lean month financially, although we were not wanting. Our grocery supply was very low, but not to the point we would starve. We knew we would not starve because God never failed us and was always supplying our needs. It was near the end of the month, and Daphne and I were discussing what we should do for supper that evening. In our discussions, our friends' name came up because we were concerned for them. We had enough to feed our family and a little bit more. We knew that our friend, his wife, and son would also be in the same predicament as us as we closed in on the end of the month. So we decided we would share some of our food with them. We surveyed the cupboards and fridge and found we had two chickens, two loaves of bread, and two pounds of margarine. It was a no-brainer. We put a chicken, a loaf of bread, and a pound of margarine in a bag and drove out to their place and gave it to them. Then we returned to our home only to find a few bags of groceries sitting on the front porch. No indication of where they came from or from whom.

This is where the sense of humor factors in. We chuckled because God had supplied abundantly once again. However, the first bag we opened had a chicken, a loaf of bread, and a pound of margarine in it. Now that's funny right there. But it was also a miracle and God's way of showing us that *everything's going to be all right!*

Lasagna Dinner

Finally, and certainly not the last, we were down to rice and bread. It was a lean time, but we knew God was not going to let us go hungry. Like I said, we had rice and bread left and little else. Undaunted by it, we set the table and just went about our usual routine. We sat at the table, and our kids thought we were crazy. We told them that God never fails, and we have this food before us, and it will be enough. Then we held hands to pray and give thanks. This is how it went: "Lord, we thank You for the food You have supplied"— *knock, knock, knock.* Someone was at the door.

I went to the door to find out who it was, and there stood a friend. In his hands was a large box. He said, "Hi, Bob. My wife wanted to know if you folks wanted to have this meal? She made lasagna and pie and stuff. I was on my way home from work, and because it is our anniversary, I made reservations at a restaurant without telling her. I called her on the way home and told her, and she said, 'What shall I do with this meal I have already made?' She then answered her own question with, 'Well, take it down to the Coutts and see if they can use it.' I went home and got it, and here I am. Can you use it?"

Lasagna dinner

Of course, I said yes and also thank you. He left, and I took the box into the dining room and set it on the table. In it were fresh hot vegetables, lasagna, apple pie, and cans of soda. We put the food on the table and proceeded to give God thanks again for supplying our need. He never fails. God heard our prayers, and our kids were amazed, and it was such a moment of teaching for them. They learned that God hears and answers prayers. They also learned that God answers in His time, not ours, and that He will grant the desire of our hearts.

Lesson

The interesting thing about miracles is that they are usually performed by God when they are needed. The timing is all in His hands. The five things I have shared with you all happened when they were needed and not a minute before. Maybe you need a miracle today. Maybe you have been waiting a while, and you are wondering if God even hears you. Let me assure you that God is in control, and He will answer you just when you need the answer. The first thing you need to do is believe that God is and that He is a rewarder of those who diligently seek Him. "But without faith it is impossible to please Him. For he that cometh to God must believe that He is, and that He is a rewarder of those who diligently seek Him" (Hebrews 11:6). All through this discourse, I have been trying to tell you that, just like me, God wants you to know that *everything's going to be all right*. So put your trust in Him and watch what God will do.

CHAPTER 9

It's All About God

College Complete

C ollege was over, and graduation ceremonies were completed, and the years that followed would fill a book of their own. From the year I graduated (1984) until I retired early because of an illness in the family in 2011, I returned to Bible college while I was pastoring and completed a master of theology and a doctor of theology. Then I pastored in home mission churches, on an Indian reservation north of the sixtieth parallel, went on mission trips, and pastored in the United States. Suffice it to say that God was in every moment of those years. I pastored, preached, married, buried, baptized, taught classes, dedicated babies, saw many, many, many miracles, and saw so many come to know Jesus as their Savior. Those years were and are special to my wife and me. It would be an injustice to them if I tried to condense them into this work, so I will consider another book at another time.

As I indicated above, I retired in 2011. I was only sixty-three, but the circumstances leading up to retirement were life-changing.

The following story is one of unexplainable miracles and the hand of God on our lives still. I will condense where I can to preserve space but not so much that we lose touch of the mighty, mighty move of God on us. It is our hope that what you read now will encourage you and uplift you in your time of need. God did things for us that are totally amazing and enough to bewilder a nonbeliever.

Daphne and I were pastoring a church in Eastern Pennsylvania, and we were right where God wanted us, and we knew it beyond a shadow of a doubt. The reason I say that is because we were on the verge of a major move of the Holy Spirit. People were getting saved and filled with the Spirit. The church was filling up. People were dancing in the Spirit, singing in tongues, waving flags, and everything was being done in order and under the direction of the Holy Spirit. In the midst of it, I felt the Lord telling me it was time to move on and let another pastor come in and take the reins and lead the revival. It was early February, and Daphne had just gone on a mission trip to India. Before she went, she had been diagnosed with liver disease. That did not stop her, and she went anyway. Then things started to happen.

300 Days

While we were in the process of deciding what we should do—or rather, what God would have us do—Daphne was getting sicker all the time due to a failing liver. Then near tragedy struck us. It was near the end of February 2011, and I walked into the room where Daphne was sitting at the computer doing some work, and I had brought her lunch. It was tacos. She ate one and wiped her mouth. The shock of what happened caused me to dial 911 immediately. There was blood all over her napkin, and she was a dark shade of gray. The ambulance came, and they took her to the emergency room. When we arrived, they took her into a room right away, and we were not there but ten minutes, and the doctor was checking her out. All of a sudden, she vomited, and she spat up eight units of blood and died on the table. The doctors shooed me out of the room and performed as they do best. Whatever they did brought her back, and they rushed her into surgery. Apparently, with liver failure, the patient is susceptible to what is called varices bleeds. Daphne had eaten the tacos, and they in turn had torn the veins which were enlarged in her throat. Not knowing she had done this, she was bleeding continuously and filled her stomach. Once she got to the hospital, it all exploded, and that was how they found out what was wrong.

In surgery, they placed bands around the veins and then put her in an induced coma where she stayed for six days. They did this so she would not do any damage to the veins while they heal. While they were doing this, I was frightened for her, and I was afraid I would lose her. I went and got on the hospital elevator and rode it up and down, talking and yelling at God. I did this more out of frustration of not knowing what was going to happen. While I was riding up and down, I finally calmed down enough to hear the voice of God speaking to me, and I distinctly heard Him say, *Bob, I told you, everything is going to be all right.* Well, it was. Six days later, they took her out of the coma; and after she gained some strength, they transferred her to the University of Pennsylvania Hospital in Philadelphia, Pennsylvania. This began a journey of 300 days in the hospital and a three-week stretch in a hospice. (No, Daphne is not gone! She is alive and well and celebrating, as of this writing, seven years with a new liver.)

The next 300 days are filled with so many moves and touches of God that I just know I will miss a few. But the purpose in sharing as much of it as I can with you is to show you that we serve a God who truly does "perfect the things that concern you," and not once did He fail, and He never will. God told me everything's going to be all right, and I believed Him and still do. While waiting for a liver, Daphne went through much turmoil in her body. She was overdosed twice in the hospital, had a colon resection, had eight compression fractures in her back, was transferred to a hospice care to die, readmitted to the hospital, and given a tune-up to try and save her for a liver. These are just a few of the many things that transpired while we waited for a liver.

Six Days to Live

Then it happened. We were nearing the end of Daphne's life, and our doctor came into our room and spoke to us in guarded terms. He said, "I am sorry to tell you, but there are just no livers available right now, especially one that matches your needs." He went on to say, "I have a suggestion for you. Call your insurance company and ask them if they would put you on the list for a liver from Florida. They have a higher turnover in that state because of the aging population." This was at eleven o'clock Friday morning.

We called the insurance company right away, and they flatly refused. They said they were not going to pay for the twenty-seven tests and procedures for Daphne to go through given the condition she was in at that moment. They said, "We are sorry, we can't help." We were devastated and totally disillusioned with insurance companies. We immediately called the doctor, who came right back. After telling him what the insurance company said, he asked me to come out of the room for a talk. Daphne was in and out of consciousness, so we went out of the room so as not to upset her. Once out of the room, the doctor informed me that he did not expect Daphne to live more than a few more days. Annette, our best friend, and I stayed in the room all weekend trying to make Daphne as comfortable as possible. It was a difficult time, and we talked to the Lord a lot.

2 a.m.!

Sunday night rolled around, and we had been talking and sleeping and watching TV all day. It was 11:00 p.m., and it was time for bed. We all took a moment and prayed and thanked God for taking care of us and again asked Him if there was a way that He would make it. Then we said good night to each other and turned out the lights. As we lay there in the dark, I lightheartedly said out of the darkness, "Wouldn't it be great if at two in the morning we got a call, and it was a new liver?" Daphne and Annette giggled and said, "That would be great." Then we went to sleep.

What I am about to tell you cannot be made up. God is on time, every time, anytime. We were sleeping, and all of a sudden, the lights went on in the room, and a nurse was standing at the door. She was very animated. She said, "Reverend Coutts, you are wanted on the telephone right away." I was still groggy but awake enough to be concerned. The first thing I did was look to my wife, thinking something had happened to her, but she was waking up, and then I thought maybe something had happened to one of my kids, and they were calling with bad news.

The nurse said, "Here, use this phone." Outside every door on the liver ward is a telephone that has a direct line to the operating room. I picked up the phone and said, "This is Reverend Coutts." On the other end was Dr. McGuire, a liver coordinator. He said, "Reverend Coutts, this is Dr. McGuire, does your wife want a new liver because I have a match here in the OR if she does?" There are thirty-five rooms on the liver floor. I looked at the clock. It was 2:00 a.m., and I hollered, "WELL YEAH!" and probably woke up all thirty-five patients on that floor.

I wept, Daphne wept, Annette wept. We laughed, we rejoiced. We knew God had a hand in it. By 8:30 a.m., Daphne was in the intensive care ward recovering. She had her new liver! Glory to God. Annette and I walked into the intensive care room, and Daphne was awake, and she had seventeen—count them, seventeen—tubes and wires coming out of her body. As we walked in, we saw that she was awake, and we simply asked, "How are you, sweetie?" She put her thumb up in the air, smiled, and passed out. She was alive, had a new liver, and on her way to recovery. All glory to God because He said, *Bob, everything's going to be all right.*

That was June 13, 2011. It would take until December 13, 2011, for her to get a final release from the hospital and sent home. We packed up our belongings and moved to Florida to a home we had purchased for a summer vacation spot. It became our permanent residence and new home. The year 2011 was long, and Daphne's road to recovery took every day. She learned to walk all over again, and slowly she got much better. Now we ride three-wheel bikes and walk a lot. Much more happened in that space of time, but again, that could possibly be another book.

From the moment of her getting out of the hospital until present day, we have never ceased to thank God for what He did. Each year on the anniversary of her transplant, we send an updated picture along with a word of thanks and encouragement to the two prominent doctors who basically saved her life at the direction of the Lord. From the time Daphne and I left the hospital in 2011 until now 2018, we have seen the hand of God on our lives literally every moment of every day. He has supplied our every need. We have been given opportunities to teach and preach and just continue on with the things of the Lord. He has led us to many new souls and given us opportunities to help them. You will remember back in this writing, I had shared a verse that has literally been the mainstay of everything, and once again I leave it with you: *"I will perfect the things that concern you. My mercy endures forever. I will not forsake the work of my hands"* (Psalms 138:8, KJV).

I would be severely remiss if I did not mention our friend Annette here. God put her in our lives. She is the most faithful friend anyone can have. When Daphne was in the hospital in Philadelphia, Annette would work all week. She would get up at 4:00 a.m., go to work for ten hours, go home, and do it four days in a row. Then Friday afternoon, she would finish work and make a three-hour drive to the hospital in Philadelphia. She would stay all weekend and help with Daphne's care; and then on Monday afternoon at 3:00 p.m., she would go home for work starting Tuesday morning. Annette did that for the whole time Daphne was in the hospital, nearly a full year. Who does that? Only someone who knows the direction of the Lord and is faithful to Him. Annette is a friend of God, and she is most definitely a friend to us. We love her beyond measure, and we pray God will bless her abundantly and beyond what she can ask or think. We love you, Annette.

So a final thought: when God says something, you can rest assured He means it and know that *everything's going to be all right.*

Everything Is Going to Be All Right

The journey God took me and my family on was not easy. What we went through, we only did with God's help. You cannot walk this kind of walk without the Lord. I am so happy I found Christ, and He walked with me the whole time. I never had to worry even though I was tempted to. Worry has a way of limiting God's work in our lives. Having faith allows God to work freely in us and do the things we think are impossible. It means untying God's hands, and that is done by having faith in Him.

If you truly want peace and assurance in your life, then the question you face is whether to have faith or to not have faith. Whatever you decide between those two options will determine your peace of mind. Otherwise, you will just live a life of worry all the time, and instead of everything being all right as God said it would, you will constantly be questioning everything.

Matthew 6:34, KJV tells us, *"Take therefore no thought for the morrow: for the morrow shall take thought for the things of itself. Sufficient unto the day is the evil thereof."*

I know it is easy to quote that verse, but to actually live it is another thing. We all have questions like, "what happens if?" or "I believe but." If you look at the last phrase in that verse, it says not to worry because today has its own problems, so don't worry about tomorrow. That is all God requires. Trust Him for today. One day at a time, and everything will be all right. God is greater than anything we can or will face.

It is unfortunate that people allow things to get to them and cause them to worry. Remember, worry is just a way to make things about ourselves and limits God from working in us. After all, God's grace is greater than any problem we will ever face. Instead of worrying, we need to believe and have faith that God is in control, and He knows what He is doing. It is so simple to live a worry-free life because a simple perusal of the Scriptures will give us direction. For instance, Matthew 6:31–33, KJV says,

> *Therefore take no thought, saying, What shall we eat? or, What shall we drink? or, Wherewithal*

shall we be clothed? For after all these things do the Gentiles seek: for your heavenly Father knoweth that ye have need of all these things. But seek ye first the kingdom of God, and his righteousness; and all these things shall be added unto you.

The answer to stress-free, worry-free living is to seek God, seek out His righteousness, and trust Him to see you through! One word from God is all you need! If you will let Him, if you will give Him a chance, He will show you His capabilities in a big way. God has no bounds when it comes to helping us. But if we don't believe that He wants to do a work in our lives, we will never give Him the freedom to go beyond what we can believe Him for!

Now unto him that is able to do exceeding abundantly above all that we ask or think, according to the power that worketh in us. (Ephesians 3:20, KJV)

Matthew Henry said, "God is able to do exceedingly, abundantly above all that we ask or think. There is an inexhaustible fullness of grace and mercy in God, which the prayers of all the saints can never draw dry. Whatever we may ask, or think to ask, God is still able to do more, abundantly more, exceedingly, abundantly more. Open thy mouth ever so wide; still he hath wherewithal to fill it. Praise God!"

So many people are aware of what God has available for them, but it seems that too many are not experiencing what's available to them? Any right-thinking person cares about the homeless and poverty level of mankind, and no one wants to go without; but when it comes to our spiritual levels, it is a different story.

When we worry and trust only in our self-effort and don't trust in God's endless capabilities, even though by the world's standards we may achieve some form of success, we are spiritually starving ourselves to death! There are a lot of spiritually malnourished Christians in this world! Anytime you rely on anything other than God, it becomes your source! Be it self, job, spouse, parents, doctors, or your own knowledge and understanding.

> *Trust in the Lord with all thine heart; and lean not unto thine own understanding. In all thy ways acknowledge him, and he shall direct thy paths. Be not wise in thine own eyes: fear the Lord, and depart from evil. It shall be health to thy navel, and marrow to thy bones. Honor the Lord with thy substance, and with the firstfruits of all thine increase: So shall thy barns be filled with plenty, and thy presses shall burst out with new wine.* (Proverbs 3:5–10, KJV)

Lean not on your own understanding. Sometimes we like to lean on everything but what we know we should. What follows now is what Daphne and I leaned on from the time we met, and through all the difficulties and trials. I certainly hope you will find comfort in them. God will make everything right in your life as well.

> *Fear not, for I am with you; be not dismayed, for I am your God; I will strengthen you, I will help you, I will uphold you with my righteous right hand.* (Isaiah 41:10, KJV)

> *Trust in the Lord with all your heart, and do not lean on your own understanding.* (Proverbs 3:5, KJV)

> *For I know the plans I have for you, declares the Lord, plans for welfare and not for evil, to give you a future and a hope. Then you will call upon me and come and pray to me, and I will hear you. You will seek me and find me, when you seek me with all your heart. I will be found by you, declares the Lord, and I will restore your fortunes and gather you*

from all the nations and all the places where I have driven you, declares the Lord, and I will bring you back to the place from which I sent you into exile. (Jeremiah 29:11–14, KJV)

And we know that for those who love God all things work together for good, for those who are called according to his purpose. (Romans 8:28, KJV)

The Lord is on my side; I will not fear. What can man do to me? The Lord is on my side as my helper; I shall look in triumph on those who hate me. It is better to take refuge in the Lord than to trust in man. It is better to take refuge in the Lord than to trust in princes. (Psalm 118:6–9, KJV)

Casting all your anxieties on him, because he cares for you. (1 Peter 5:7, KJV)

I can do all things through him who strengthens me. (Philippians 4:13, KJV)

The Lord is my shepherd; I shall not want. He makes me lie down in green pastures. He leads me beside still waters. He restores my soul. He leads me in paths of righteousness for his name's sake. Even though I walk through the valley of the shadow of death, I will fear no evil, for you are with me; your rod and your staff, they comfort me. You prepare a table before me in the presence of my enemies; you anoint my head with oil; my cup overflows. (Psalm 23:1–6, KJV)

For I consider that the sufferings of this present time are not worth comparing with the glory that is to be revealed to us. (Romans 8:18, KJV)

We are afflicted in every way, but not crushed; perplexed, but not driven to despair; persecuted, but not forsaken; struck down, but not destroyed; always carrying in the body the death of Jesus, so that the life of Jesus may also be manifested in our bodies. For we who live are always being given over to death for Jesus' sake, so that the life of Jesus also may be manifested in our mortal flesh. So death is at work in us, but life in you. (2 Corinthians 4:8–18, KJV)

Put on the whole armor of God, that you may be able to stand against the schemes of the devil. (Ephesians 6:11, KJV)

Therefore I tell you, do not be anxious about your life, what you will eat or what you will drink, nor about your body, what you will put on. Is not life more than food, and the body more than clothing? (Matthew 6:25, KJV)

For I know the plans I have for you, declares the Lord, plans for welfare and not for evil, to give you a future and a hope. (Jeremiah 29:11, KJV)

But they who wait for the Lord shall renew their strength; they shall mount up with wings like eagles; they shall run and not be weary; they shall walk and not faint. (Isaiah 40:31, KJV)

For we walk by faith, not by sight. (2 Corinthians 5:7, KJV)

I sought the Lord, and he answered me and delivered me from all my fears. (Psalm 34:4, KJV)

Blessed is the man who walks not in the counsel of the wicked, nor stands in the way of sinners, nor sits in the seat of scoffers; but his delight is in the law of the Lord, and on his law he meditates day and night. He is like a tree planted by streams of water that yields its fruit in its season, and its leaf does not wither. In all that he does, he prospers. (Psalm 1:1–3, KJV)

As we look not to the things that are seen but to the things that are unseen. For the things that are seen are transient, but the things that are unseen are eternal. (2 Corinthians 4:18, KJV)

Keep your life free from love of money, and be content with what you have, for he has said, "I will never leave you nor forsake you." (Hebrews 13:5, KJV)

My son, do not forget my teaching, but let your heart keep my commandments, for length of days and years of life and peace they will add to you. Let not steadfast love and faithfulness forsake you; bind them around your neck; write them on the tablet of your heart. So you will find favor and good success in the sight of God and man. Trust in the Lord with all your heart, and do not lean on your own understanding. (Proverbs 3:1–6, KJV)

Peace I leave with you; my peace I give to you. Not as the world gives do I give to you. Let not your hearts be troubled, neither let them be afraid. (John 14:27, KJV)

All the paths of the Lord are steadfast love and faithfulness, for those who keep his covenant and his testimonies. (Psalm 25:10, KJV)

Now to him who is able to do far more abundantly than all that we ask or think, according to the power at work within us, to him be glory in the church and in Christ Jesus throughout all generations, forever and ever. Amen. (Ephesians 3:20–21, KJV)

Do not be anxious about anything, but in everything by prayer and supplication with thanksgiving let your requests be made known to God. (Philippians 4:6, KJV)

For God so loved the world, that he gave his only Son, that whoever believes in him should not perish but have eternal life. (John 3:16, KJV)

Be still, and know that I am God. I will be exalted among the nations, I will be exalted in the earth! (Psalm 46:10, KJV)

I have said these things to you, that in me you may have peace. In the world you will have tribulation. But take heart; I have overcome the world. (John 16:33, KJV)

Have I not commanded you? Be strong and courageous. Do not be frightened, and do not be dismayed, for the Lord your God is with you wherever you go. (Joshua 1:9, KJV)

Behold, the Lord's hand is not shortened, that it cannot save, or his ear dull, that it cannot hear. (Isaiah 59:1, KJV)

Be strong and courageous. Do not fear or be in dread of them, for it is the Lord your God who goes with you. He will not leave you or forsake you. (Deuteronomy 31:6, KJV)

Do not be anxious about anything, but in everything by prayer and supplication with thanksgiving let your requests be made known to God. And the peace of God, which surpasses all understanding, will guard your hearts and your minds in Christ Jesus. (Philippians 4:6–7, KJV)

For God so loved the world, that he gave his only Son, that whoever believes in him should not perish but have eternal life. For God did not send his Son into the world to condemn the world, but in order that the world might be saved through him. (John 3:16–17, KJV)

Blessed is the man who remains steadfast under trial, for when he has stood the test he will receive the crown of life, which God has promised to those who love him. (James 1:12, KJV)

But seek first the kingdom of God and his righteousness, and all these things will be added to you. (Matthew 6:33, KJV)

You keep him in perfect peace whose mind is stayed on you, because he trusts in you. Trust in the Lord forever, for the Lord God is an everlasting rock. (Isaiah 26:3–4, KJV)

And I am sure of this, that he who began a good work in you will bring it to completion at the day of Jesus Christ. (Philippians 1:6, KJV)

For God gave us a spirit not of fear but of power and love and self-control. (2 Timothy 1:7, KJV)

You keep him in perfect peace whose mind is stayed on you, because he trusts in you. (Isaiah 26:3, KJV)

Let us hold fast the confession of our hope without wavering, for he who promised is faithful. (Hebrews 10:23, KJV)

Finally, brothers, whatever is true, whatever is honorable, whatever is just, whatever is pure, whatever is lovely, whatever is commendable, if there is any excellence, if there is anything worthy of praise, think about these things. (Philippians 4:8, KJV)

Before I formed you in the womb I knew you, and before you were born I consecrated you; I appointed you a prophet to the nations. (Jeremiah 1:5, KJV)

In all your ways acknowledge him, and he will make straight your paths. (Proverbs 3:6, KJV)

Delight yourself in the Lord, and he will give you the desires of your heart. (Psalm 37:4, KJV)

Therefore, since we are surrounded by so great a cloud of witnesses, let us also lay aside every weight, and sin which clings so closely, and let us run with endurance the race that is set before us. (Hebrews 12:1, KJV)

Jesus said to him, "I am the way, and the truth, and the life. No one comes to the Father except through me." (John 14:6, KJV)

And without faith it is impossible to please him, for whoever would draw near to God must believe that he exists and that he rewards those who seek him. (Hebrews 11:6, KJV)

For we are his workmanship, created in Christ Jesus for good works, which God prepared beforehand, that we should walk in them. (Ephesians 2:10, KJV)

You will not fear the terror of the night, nor the arrow that flies by day, nor the pestilence that stalks in darkness, nor the destruction that wastes at noonday. A thousand may fall at your side, ten thousand at your right hand, but it will not come near you. You will only look with your eyes and see the recompense of the wicked. Because you have made the Lord your dwelling place—the Most High, who is my refuge. (Psalm 91:5–10, KJV)

EPILOGUE

What is an epilogue? An epilogue is a section or speech at the end of a book or play that serves as a comment on or a conclusion to what has happened.

Well, we have come to the end of this book, and now is the time to sum things up for you. When I was a young boy, God told me everything was going to be all right. The abuse was horrible; it was part of my life for obvious reasons I did not describe it all. There is no glory in it for anyone. The separation from my family was heartbreaking but a learning curve. A learning curve in that I was able, over the years, to see God put a plan together that would boggle the normal mind. I and my family went through trials, crisis, sickness, pain, separation, and many more negatives than I care to count. However, He was present in each one, and He showed Himself real each time.

My life started off being an abused kid. How did it end? Well, that is the subject of this epilogue. I want to deliver to you a short story that absolutely shows that when God says everything will be all right, He means it. After nearly forty years of no contact with my father (except for a brief five minutes in 1975 when I went to his house to pick up my sister and another one hour in 1977 when Daphne and I were on our way to Bible college and stopped to see if I might be able to talk to him and let him know I had become a Christian and was going to be a minister), I received an e-mail which was forwarded to me from someone else. My sister whom I had not had close contact with for a few years felt I should be made aware that my father was not in the best of health, and if I were interested, I could contact her for more information.

Interested? Do birds fly? Yes, I was interested. I made contact within minutes, and also within minutes, a reply came, which set the wheels in motion. My sister and I hooked up by telephone, and within minutes, we had caught up on lost time between us. Her name is Mary, and Mary made contact with my father to see if he would be willing to see me if I made my way to Vancouver Island, which is on the west coast of Canada.

The first thing that needed to fall into place was me. I needed to sort out in my head if this is what I wanted to do or not. It took me a few weeks of praying and seeking God to get clarity. Finally, I believe God spoke to my heart, and it was settled in my heart: I would go. Many things needed to fall into place before I could go. Airfare had to be right. Time away from my pastoral duties needed approval. Speakers needed to be lined up. And most of all, my father needed to say yes, he would see me. Within hours, Mary had been to see my father, and he said yes, he wanted to see me. So I made the arrangements to go, and before I left, the church I was pastoring prayed for me. I welcomed that because of the emotions I was feeling.

Now, before I go any further, I want you to know, forgiveness has always been in my heart for my father and what he did to me as I grew up. I had dealt with it years before when Jesus dealt with me about forgiveness, and He extended His grace to me. So praying was to make sure I was going with the right mind-set. God cleared that up for me. What follows is the exciting story of how, after nearly forty years of estrangement, God made everything all right again. The best way to explain this story is to narrate it and show you the proof in pictures, which will explain what my Lord has done.

The first picture I am going to show you, you have already seen in the book. It is a picture of Dad when he was in the Royal Canadian Air Force and I was a young boy. It was a terrible time in my life, and as you can tell from the picture, he was a very strict-looking man. I felt the brunt of that strictness often and wished I could forget it.

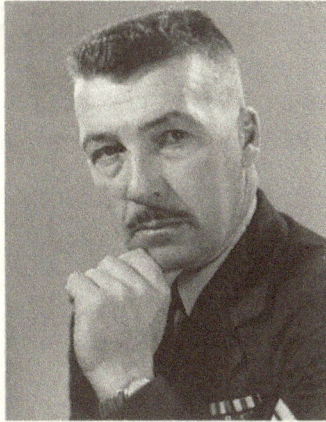

George R. Coutts (my dad),1920–2008

This picture was taken in 1956. I was eight years old, and it was probably the most awful time of my life. My father was heavily into alcohol. He abused me in every way imaginable—physically, mentally, and even sexually—all because of his penchant for booze, which made him a mean, aggressive, and vengeful drunk. This picture to me is the epitome of anger. That anger was invariably taken out on me.

However, anger and abuse aside, something happened to me when I turned eleven years old. I accepted Jesus as my Savior, and I had a vision or epiphany if you will. In it, Jesus came to me (spiritually speaking, of course), and He told me, "Bobby, everything is going to be all right," and He was right. Through a series of events outlined in the book, I ended up on my own, and eventually in the '70s, God placed a call on my life to become a minister in His service. It was 1968 when I last had contact with him as outlined in the book. I saw Mom at the same time for about five minutes in 1977, and that was the last time I ever saw her or spoke to her. I found out in 2000 that she had died in 1999.

Now fast-forward to 2008. After hearing from my sister Mary and getting all the logistics sorted out, I found myself walking down the hallway of the hospital on Vancouver Island on the other side of the continent. I was walking down the hall toward my father's room. I was walking toward his room in fear and trepidation. I saw a short man whom I honestly did not recognize at first. He was shorter than I remember. It was my father. He was frail and even looked a little bewildered. As I got nearer to him, he looked directly at me and said these words. "What took you so long to get here?"

He was old, frail, and a little confused.

I walked over to him, and he put his hand on my shoulder, and I put mine on his, and I said to him, "Dad, I came out here in fear and trepidation, not knowing how you would receive me." He said, "Bob, I was worried as well, not knowing if you would really come, and if you did, how you would receive me as well."

Once we greeted each other and opened up a conversation, we embraced, and Dad said this: "I hope yesterday is gone, Bob. It should not have taken this long for us to get back together."

I agreed with my father, and as you can see from the next picture, there was a release for the two of us.

A genuine release

But that was not even the best part! The next picture I am going to show you is a completely different father than I remember.

I remember the severe alcoholism that caused the horrible temper to be lashed out on me. I remember the fear, the abuse, the loneliness, and the rejection, but now something was different, not because he was older but because his facial expression was so completely different from the day he told me to get out of his sight forever.

When I became a Christian and told my father I was going to be a minister of the Gospel, he told me I needed to denounce that notion, my faith, and become a Mason in his Masonic lodge. He said if I did not, I should get out of his life before he did what was required of him. He wanted me to join his Masonic lodge and become a Mason as he was because, to him, Masons and ministry were diametrically opposed to each other, so he said.

My father was very high up in the Masonic order, so he needed to distance himself from me unless I joined. Hence the decision I was faced, which caused him much grief because I chose Jesus over the Masons; and in the end, he had told me to get out of his life. But now there was something different about my father, and I needed to ask him what it was.

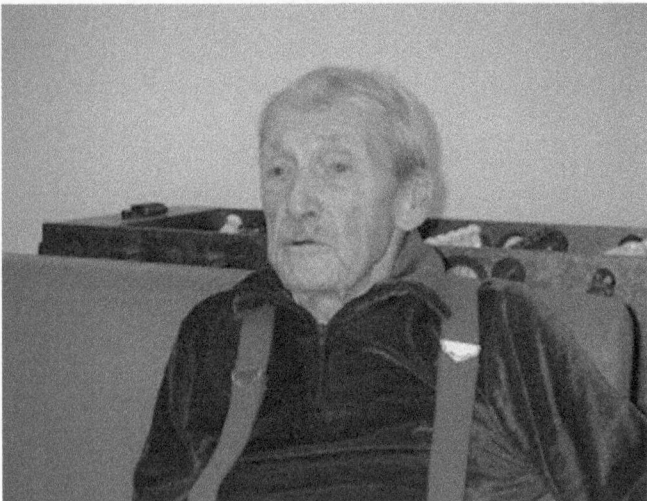

Something was different.

So here is Dad sitting and talking with me. I had just asked him a question about what was going on with him and why did he look so different because I was mesmerized by his countenance. My father gave me a one-word answer that literally took my breath away and left me totally speechless. My question to him was this: "Dad, what is it about you? You look so different." He simply said, "Jesus." Like a fool, I said, "What?" Then my father said, "Jesus changed me. I was a drunk and a fool. I have asked Jesus to forgive me and to help me right all the wrong I ever did to my family. I have been asking Him every night for almost two years to help me." He went on to say, "I left the Masons two years ago, and I have not had a drop of booze in those two years. Jesus is helping me and forgiving me. I let the booze come between you and I. Can you ever forgive me?" You could have knocked me over with a feather at that very moment, and of course, I said *yes*, and I also asked my father to forgive me. He did!

Born again and forgiveness flowing!

He said yes, and that set off a time of rejoicing like I never imagined. I never dreamed I would ever see my father again, let alone see him with Christ in his life. Next I asked Dad to do something more out of a need for my own heart's satisfaction than out of disbelief. I asked him if I could hear him say the sinner's prayer with my sister Mary and me. He agreed, and we did.

God is amazing. But again, that was not all. Dad blew me away again. He said, "Bob do you remember that Jacob and Esau thing in the Bible where the father passed on the blessing?" I said, "Yes, I know the story." He said, "When you went away, I vowed to never lay eyes on you again. As far as I was concerned, you were dead to me. As I look at it now, I realize that was a curse and not a blessing. Would you mind if I passed on a belated father's blessing to you now?" I was speechless. He put his hand on my shoulder and said, "Son, I am proud of what you have become, and I would like to pass on a blessing to you in your life and work in the name of Jesus. Go in peace!" I received my father's blessing. This from a man who vowed to have nothing ever to do with me again. A man who said, as far as he was concerned, I was dead to him, and now he was passing on a blessing to me. God is awesome.

After my father passed on the blessing to me, he grabbed my hand and said, "Never again will I allow myself to be separated from you or the rest of the family except by death, and I know that will only be for a while." God is amazing. You would think that would be enough miracles for one day, but no. There was one more. After I spent a few days visiting with my father and catching up on all the lost years, it was time to go home. When I left, my father said good-bye in four words. They are the four words I have never heard in all my growing years right up until this moment with him—which, at the time of my visit, would have been sixty years. And I want you to know that I am dead serious when I tell you in those sixty years, these four words have never crossed his lips to me. He said, "I love you, Bob." And we parted. They were the last words ever spoken between us. Dad passed away shortly thereafter. God is a miracle-working God.

That, folks, is the epilogue to this book. From a life of abuse as a young boy to ministry to restoration with my father—and God's hand on me and my family the whole time. Is there any question the statement God made is true? *Everything is going to be all right!* "And all through the book you can see God fulfilled his promise. *"For I know the plans I have for you," declares the Lord, "plans to prosper you and not to harm you, plans to give you hope and a future."* Jeremiah 29:11, KJV. God is doing just that for Daphne and I and he will do the same for you."

Rev. Dr. Robert and Daphne Coutts

Daphne and I hope that what you have read in these pages will touch your heart in such a way that it encourages you. It is our prayer, first of all, that if you do not know Jesus Christ as your personal Savior, you will take time today to say the sinner's prayer and invite Jesus into your heart. Romans 10:9–10 says that "if you declare with your mouth, 'Jesus is Lord,' and believe in your heart that God raised him from the dead, you will be saved. For it is with your heart that you believe and are justified, and it is with your mouth that you profess your faith and are saved." Ask Him to forgive you of your sins today, and He will. He will wash you and make you clean and assure you of a place in heaven. Pray this prayer today:

> Dear Lord Jesus, I know that I am a sinner, and
> I ask for Your forgiveness. I believe You died for

my sins and rose from the dead. I turn from my
sins and invite You to come into my heart and
life. I want to trust and follow You as my Lord
and Savior. In Your name, amen.

Secondly, if you are struggling with the way your life is taking
you, take heart because, as you can see by the stories in these pages,
God has it under control, and He is guiding your life as He promised
all of us He would do. May you be blessed today and forever.

ABOUT THE AUTHOR

Rev. Dr. Robert Stephen James Coutts

Robert Coutts is an Assemblies of God minister, semiretired, and living with his beautiful wife, Daphne, in the sunny state of Florida. Robert began his pastoral calling in Canada and eventually moved to the United States, where he and his wife became permanent residents. They have lived and pastored in the USA for eighteen years. Robert still fills in as a supply preacher and helps out in the church wherever he is needed. Roberts's wife received a liver transplant in 2011, precipitating his retirement from full-time to part-time ministry so that he would be able to care for his wife. God has been more than faithful to both of them, and they serve Him out of a deep love for how God cares for them.

As a youngster, Robert began his life's journey in an abusive home. Being raised in an atmosphere of alcohol and violence did little to keep fear and anger from taking total control of his life until one eventful night when he had an epiphany. God appeared to him in what Robert now says was more than likely a dream, although it felt good that God came right into his room. That dream changed everything for him because at that moment, the Lord spoke to him and told him that *everything was going to be all right*. It was.

God planted a verse in Roberts's heart that proved God was leading: "'For I know the plans I have for you,' declares the LORD, 'plans to prosper you and not to harm you, plans to give you hope and a future'" (Jeremiah 29:11, NIV). Gradually, life changed, and Robert was led to a saving knowledge of Jesus, and a life of one miracle after another followed. God led Robert to a wife through near-death sickness, Bible college, and then nearly losing a wife. But God was always there. All along the way, Robert heard the statement over and over, "Everything is going to be all right." With God leading, Robert came to understand that no matter the circumstance, no matter what the calamity, everything truly will be all right when a person leans solely on the Lord. The life of abuse and separation Robert faced has come full circle to a life of freedom and forgiveness. God changed everything, and Robert has shared that by bearing his heart in these pages. It is done, he says, in hopes that others will hear the message of God that *everything is going to be all right*.

CPSIA information can be obtained
at www.ICGtesting.com
Printed in the USA
FFHW020137110719
53565639-59218FF

9 781645 154761